Dear Mum

Dear Mum

Edited by
SAMUEL JOHNSON OAM

Illustrated by
SHAUN TAN

hachette
AUSTRALIA

hachette
AUSTRALIA

Published in Australia and New Zealand in 2021
by Hachette Australia
(an imprint of Hachette Australia Pty Limited)
Level 17, 207 Kent Street, Sydney NSW 2000
www.hachette.com.au

10 9 8 7 6 5 4 3 2 1

Copyright © Love Your Sister 2021

A catalogue record for this
book is available from the
National Library of Australia

ISBN: 978 0 7336 4593 8 (hardback)

Cover and internal design by Christabella Designs
Cover and internal illustrations by Shaun Tan
Typeset in Garamond Regular by Kirby Jones
Printed and bound in Australia by McPherson's Printing Group

MIX
Paper from
responsible sources
FSC® C001695

The paper this book is printed on is certified against the
Forest Stewardship Council® Standards. McPherson's
Printing Group holds FSC® chain of custody certification
SA-COC-005379. FSC® promotes environmentally
responsible, socially beneficial and economically viable
management of the world's forests.

Contents

A message from the editor

All we need is love. At the centre of love is families. At the centre of families is mums. This collection of letters is dedicated to all the mums out there.

Thank you for all the mumming.

Samuel Johnson OAM

Dear Mum

You'll perhaps consider me a little slipshod opening my letter this way. But it is my letter, and it is my opinion that this correspondence should begin with your words, for yours are so much better.

Softball Match at the Tech School

Frangar
Chook
Fuckerata
Susie Babe
Danger
Fungoid Fool
Anderson's dick, you can't find it,
Pig's ring
Bullcrap
Stick your arse behind the backstop and
Shut yer mouth

Four balls make a walk
He stole the whole base
Miss; Miss.
We wanna go home
Strike one for Fatty
Over there
This kid's trying to kill me
Murder you
Fuck you
Take it easy.

I love that poem. I would love to write one back, but I'm a shit poet.

It feels odd writing to you. I don't know much about you really. I don't know where or when you were born, or when you died. I don't know your middle name or what colour you wore your hair. I thought you might be interested to hear what I do know of you though, for there is much you've missed.

I lived above Dad's second-hand bookshop for years. When I was fifteen, having abandoned my dreams of tennis, of Wimbledon, I started working at becoming a bohemian of considerable import. I didn't know a great deal about poetry but I'd somehow surmised I wouldn't be able to call myself a true bohemian if I didn't sport at least a rudimentary grasp. I wore my beret, but it was starting to feel false. And so, in search of authenticity, I trundled down our rickety wooden spiral staircase into Dad's bookshop and its poetry section. I found you in the first book I picked out – an anthology of Australian women poets published in the '70s, called *Mother, I'm Rooted*. I picked it up because it had the word 'rooted' on the cover. I was fifteen; it figures. I opened the book square on 'Softball Match at the Tech School' and I was in at fungoid fool. You used your words bravely, leaving me giddy and confused. You put pictures in my head and made me laugh and then feel sad straight after. You captured me with your vivid wordplays and punctuated musicality. I hungered for more than your six poems in the anthology. I searched for you in the index of every other book in the section and found nothing. But I had a piece of you. And I could now attest to being a legitimate bohemian, having been so greatly moved by your lyrical dexterity. I donned my beret free of guilt, before taking my customary walk along the beach. To think. And smoke cigarettes. Because that's what fifteen-year-old bohemians do.

Over the years I'd hear talk of you. Sometimes I'd fossick and sometimes I'd happen upon it. Apparently, you went mad. Too much acid. By all accounts you found life a most dreadful and onerous undertaking, which I think I understand. Despite this, you held famed parties where you would invite the street urchins and the upper classes, just to watch the fireworks. I learnt that you believed in God most fervently, but I can only assume that you shared a tempestuous bond in light of your purported behaviour being so rarely in line with Bible principles. I heard you fed your preschool daughter LSD to open her mind.

When you weren't in the housing commissions you were in the institutions. They don't exist anymore, you might be interested to know. I heard you reached for God when you got lost but he wasn't there. In amongst it all, I'm told you had three kids and married a bloke and it didn't work out. I heard that you loved him more than he loved you, and that it broke

3

your heart. But I'm told there were lots of things that broke your heart. I'm told that you finally ended it after countless attempts.

You don't know this, and this is why I'm writing to you, but you came into my home when I was nineteen. Generally speaking, my memory is patchy, but I remember this day like no other and you feature in it most prominently. I was back for another stint above Dad's bookshop, another effort to reshuffle my ruffled affairs. I had left the bohemian thing behind, realising that only wankers wore berets, and was dedicated to becoming a fully-fledged cynic. I was depressed because the world was like your poems, oddly enough. The one thing holding me together was family and, thankfully, I had care of my nephew Jonathon that day. Young Jonno had been tasked with some creative writing homework. He had to write a story. Dad had encouraged me to write stories from a very early age and he kept every story I ever wrote in his filing cabinet, hoping, as any old book dealer might, that his son would be the next Proust. Regardless, there was one story I had written, when I was about Jonno's age, called 'The Old Man and the Watermelon' and I thought I might read it to Jonno in an effort to somehow inspire him, such was my hubris at that age.

As I rifled through Dad's filing cabinet, I came across a tab that read 'Merrill's Poems'.

There you were again.

My heart faltered. I couldn't deal with it while Jonno was up. I sequestered the file in my room before finding 'The Old Man and the Watermelon' and reading it. Jonno wrote his piece, we had apple pie and custard, he brushed his teeth,

I read him another chunk of *Huck Finn* and tucked him away safe and sound. I sat in my bedroom. I fingered the manila folder nervously, not sure I was ready to see what was inside. It felt wrong to be reading a private file of my father's, but he need not ever know. There were maybe a hundred poems. I turned the pages slowly, edging ever closer to knowing you. I drifted through your twisted mind. Your pages were lyrical, alarming, completely disconnected, manic, paranoid, sinister, even graceful, depending on the day or your mood or your place. In no time flat, there were only two pages left unread. I searched the penultimate page for a title, but this was the first poem without one. It just said, simply and in brackets, (For Samuel Joseph). That's my name. You wrote a poem for me. Before you died. Now you weren't some acid-drenched poet. Now you were my mum. I'm writing to tell you that I found the poem you wrote me. You've probably forgotten it, so here it is:

(For Samuel Joseph)

When 'this old man'
From the nursery rhyme
Rolled home
You were hiding in his sack and
Seizing the first gruff moment his back
Was turned you stuck your head
Out and grinned

O lord how I sinned
No great sin to conceive
You little son, receive

A mother's prayer for you
And a fresh pair of pants
Gold ducks on red overalls

Little fellow fat tum
With your chest all a rumble
Go cough in the night
Look look see the thumb
Making arcs in the air by the
Window is your own
Thumb and the fingers
Leave the fingers weaving
Greetings to the pane
And smile just once again
Forever for your
Once and for all mum

If I'd lost you big bonny baby son
Sam Sam listen if you can Sam
There'd never be another son
Like you so

I sent the silly fellow from the rhyme a
Packing, skulking off with nought
But empty sacking for company
And I kept you
Treasure devil dear

All the seas of joy
Rise to sing for you boy
Surge and swell and roar
All the seas of joy
Sound wonderfully near
Since you've been here

I wrote to you not just to tell you that I found your poem, and to thank you for it, but in some feeble hope that perhaps, like me, you'll find this letter buried in a filing cabinet somewhere. And so you know who your son is, there are a few things I need to make clear.

I've become a half-decent human. There's a miscreant in me and I've fucked up plenty, but I've balanced out my base hedonism with sizeable helpings of community work and I endeavour to be the best that I can. They told me I have what you had but I don't believe them, and I've been off my medication for nearly eight years without incident. I've never tried to kill myself. I'm a practising minimalist and your poem is one of my few possessions, protected in fireproof glass. I give most of what I earn to my family and loved ones and am generous with my time. I'm not particularly good at any one thing but I try hard and I'm proud of that. I think you tried hard too. Maybe that's where I got it. Despite mostly feeling that my life has been an unending series of fuck-ups, I've found some confidence and a little security, in so far as you can.

I have never blamed you for leaving. Lots of people these days call suicide selfish. They say, what about the kids? What about the family? Not realising it's not at all about them. I don't miss you, for I never had you to miss. That bloke you had three kids with stepped up when you stepped out. He was effeminate and authoritative, so I had a two-in-one type of deal. I'm pretty much okay, except I have intimacy issues and I can't share a bed. I feel lucky that you didn't stick around and fuck up my life like you did my sister's. Hilde found you dead when she was twelve. She was late to see you. Ever since, she's carried a swag of neuroses. She's never once been late in the decades since. Thanks for making her so punctual. I've only seen one photo of us together. I've never cared to obtain my own copy. You were cremated, but the small plaque with your name on it is long lost and only your punctual daughter has ever searched for it. To be honest, for that's what letters ought be, I think I did better without you. I think you knew I would. You are mostly forgotten now, which happens of course, but your poetry stays near and that is your gift.

With true thanks, for changing my life for the better, forever, from your, once and for all, big bonny baby son,

Samuel Joseph

Samuel Johnson OAM: Gold Logie and AFI Award-winning actor, winner of Dancing with the Stars*, long-distance unicyclist and Head of Cancer Vanquishment at Love Your Sister*

Dear Mum

It was all a bit much, wasn't it.

Hilde

Hilde Hinton: author, prison officer and Love Your Sister co-founder

Dear Mum

The older I get the more aware I am of how you influenced my life.

The positive modelling I received as one of four children, who all sat around the family table with you, Dad and Grandpa has made me convinced that this is the best way to create food lovers for life. Not only were you a curious and creative cook but you subtly opened my sensibilities as well as my tastebuds. In a family with little spare cash you still embroidered table mats, selected pretty bowls and platters to put the food on, made your own dinner rolls and topped them with poppy seeds or sesame seeds. We always had cloth napkins, never paper. We always had butter on a butter dish, never a plastic box on our table, and you always told us the stories that went with the dishes.

We also learnt about caring for the ducks, and how to pick fruit. I suspect we could have been more helpful in the digging and turning the compost, but we knew it was happening.

You also invited others to share our table often and made simple meals into celebrations.

I suspect you were not really surprised that I opened a restaurant, nor that I started to write about the stories behind my dishes.

Sadly, you were not there to see me take my next big step to create the experiment that has become the Stephanie Alexander Kitchen Garden Foundation. Thousands of Australian children are now learning about growing, harvesting, preparing and sharing fresh food in the most enjoyable way – a hands-on program that is rapidly spreading through our schools and early learning centres.

I still think of you every day and I know that all that I learnt from you is still being passed on to others.

Thanks Mum

Stephanie

Stephanie Alexander AO: owner–chef, author, food educator and founder of the Stephanie Alexander Kitchen Garden Foundation

Dear Mum

There are still times when I go to call you.

It seems inexplicable to me that you actually died. I used to wonder how it would feel, and after sixteen years, I'm still not sure.

The main thing I want to tell you is that I get it now. I understand that all those times I thought you were smothering or controlling were all just manifestations of love. And I hope my boys will one day understand the same of me.

Liam left home at the beginning of the year to begin his university life, and I fell to pieces. I was right back to being seventeen and leaving home for uni myself. Had I even given you and Dad a backward glance? Had I an iota of insight into how you were feeling as I left my childhood behind? Did you find it hard to let me go? I missed you terribly as I cried over Liam's departure.

And the clothes you made me to take away? I was embarrassed by the Butterick patterns and homemade jumpers. I wanted to shop at the army disposal store. I felt you didn't 'see' me. But I now know that love is a doing word, and every trip to the fabric department of Myer was an act of love.

Jack was so young when you died. You would have laughed at the boys at your 'ceremony'. (I know you didn't want a funeral.) Liam dragged Jack around the floor by his arms. A nice diversion on the hardest of days. When Jack was five he said, 'I wish I knew Grandma when I had a brain.' Me too. You'd just love these boys … actually they are now fine young men. And I tell them often how proud you'd be of their achievements.

I find it hard to talk about you without getting weepy (I'm crying writing this). I get a kick to the heart if I see your handwriting, and despite the fact you didn't like having your photo taken I have your pictures all over the house. Most importantly I want you to know that your determination for me to have an education and pursue a career has afforded me a wonderful and challenging life, and I hope I do you credit.

And I miss you every day. (Sorry to begin a sentence with 'and'.)

Love

Amanda x

Amanda Keller OAM: award-winning journalist and the Hostess with the Mostess; Jonesy and Amanda, Dancing with the Stars, The Living Room. *Amanda appears daily, in wax, at Madame Tussauds in Sydney.*

Dear Mum

Remember when I went away for work with my son Hakavai, and you came along to help out? It was the end of a three week trip and I was exhausted, Hakavai was irritated, and your perpetual enthusiasm was excruciating.

We were slowly walking up the boardwalk, only one plane ride away until touchdown in Sydney.

'Mum, where are our seats?' I asked.

'How should I know?!' you replied in a haughty tone.

'Um … you've got the boarding passes.'

You peered down through your glasses (bought at the chemist down the road). I knew you couldn't read our seat numbers.

'Here, give them to me,' I said.

'No,' you huffed back. As if to prove to me that you could indeed read, you made the following announcement in your boombox supersonic circus ringmaster voice.

'Masterrrrr Hakavai Hoskin – seatttt 25AAAAAAAAA!!!'

The other passengers jumped, startled by your announcement.

We moved to our seats and while I got Hakavai settled, I saw you had spotted a new friend in the flight attendant (not the same one you were talking to earlier, the one you thought was Polish, but was actually from Serbia).

I tuned in to your conversation in time and heard you playfully admonish him, 'I'm not from New Zealand, I'm from Tahiti!' Your face had that focused intensity I know so well.

'That is fascinating, Madam.'

His body language, tone of voice and lack of any expression indicated that he was anything but fascinated.

'Ah, so where is that?' he added with a modicum of polite interest.

'In French Polynesia of course! Everybody should know where French Polynesia is!'

(Because of COURSE everyone should know the exact location of some islands sprinkled around the Pacific Ocean?)

'My uncle was president of Tahiti. Three times!' you exclaimed, with a knowing smile.

(I'm still not sure if this is factually correct as you seem to find an ancestral connection to almost everyone from Tahiti.)

'Ahhhhhh ...' he looked at me through 'Help me!' eyes and I pretended to be busy reading. I wanted to see how this was going to play out.

'Yes!' you proclaimed. 'Us Tahitians, we're proud of our culture!'

Then, just as I saw you draw a big breath, ready to launch into your next verbal barrage, there was an announcement over the PA and the flight attendant's shoulders sank with relief.

'Please excuse me Madam, we're about to take off.'

'Oh! No worries darling!' You stood to kiss him but he was already moving quickly down the aisle.

'*Māuruuru Māuruuru roa!*' you called after him, quickly adding, 'That means thank you in Tahitian!'

You settled back in your seat and started tickling my son's feet. He giggled, enraptured by your clinking shell necklaces and the daisies in your hair. Your chignon was held up with an old ballpoint pen, you were wearing a vibrant floral shirt, and psychedelic patterned tights.

Awwww. I was suddenly overwhelmed by feelings of love and gratitude for you. I was a bit of a bitch to you on that trip. I thought about when I was a kid, and you took me to a big running race. I thought of the time when I won an award for my colourful imagination and you bought me an old clunky typewriter. I remembered when I was in hospital, and you were there every day, brightening up the place with your florid colours and raucous laughter.

I grabbed your hand and kissed it.

'Love ya, Mum.'

You smiled at me, and kissed my hand too.

Turia

Turia Pitt: bestselling author, athlete and mindset coach

Dear Mum

It's been a long time since I've written you a letter.

And even longer since you've been able to read one.

I can only imagine what it's like for you in there, especially knowing the person you were before.

Sometimes I still see the 'you' I grew up with. Although I haven't actually seen you in person for over two years now. Just photos that Helen from the Alzheimer's Ward sends me.

I think of all the times you told me you never wanted to end up a 'bloody vegetable'. How, if it ever came to that, I had your permission to 'knock you on the head'.

Instead, I just let you sit in your nursing home, like a piece of broccoli simmering away on a stove longer than it should.

And to think I had the chance to pull the plug once.

After you broke your hip in March 2015, just two months after my wife buggered off, and one month after my dog died and I was slightly consumed with grief, the doctor at the hospital in Geelong emerged from the operating theatre to tell me you were struggling with aspiration and it would take some doing for you to fully recover. After explaining a few different procedures and inquiring about your quality of life he then asked me what I wanted him to do.

Why was he asking me? I'm not a doctor.

In my ignorance, I took it to mean he wanted my permission to do what he could to keep you alive. It wasn't until my newly ex-wife's father (a doctor himself) explained to me your doctor was very subtly hinting at something else. That should it seem a better course of action to just 'let you go' he would, in fact, do nothing other than the usual hip replacement recovery business, and you would likely 'kick the bucket'.

That would've been your preferred option. It was certainly one of your favourite expressions.

So … you're still here. But of course – not really. Cruel. A failure on my part. And now I must watch from half a world away as you ever so slowly drift further into the abyss.

It's funny when I think of how short and sharp Dad's death was. A shocking flight accident that killed him instantly. Whereas your demise is, as Fiona Apple would say, 'Slow like honey. Heavy with mood.'

I'm sorry, Mum. I'm sorry your doctor was offering you a way out and I didn't see it. I'm sorry you now must endure more years of oblivion, instead of being reunited with your precious love – my dad, taken from you 44 years ago. I'm just sorry. I often picture that scene from *One Flew Over the Cuckoo's Nest*. You know the one. With the pillow …

You'll probably outlive me. You're going to be 85 this Christmas. Here's to another ten years of Alzheimer's. At least I can give you the same present I gave you three years ago.

I'll just take it down off your shelf and hand it to you again. I know the old you would find that quite funny.

But you're not the old you anymore. That you – the smart, sarcastic, stoic woman who taught me to keep my chin up and my head down – only lives on in my memory.

I share stories with Monte about you. I want him to know what kind of lady you were. I think he's getting the idea. He just turned four and has quite the sense of humour. I gather that's yours being passed down. I wonder if he'll understand what the doctor is hinting at when my time comes to get a hip replacement. Being from the Netherlands he probably will.

I love you Mum. More and more all the time. I'm sorry for making you stay, longer than you should.

I'm coming home later this year.

I'll be sure to bring a lovely soft new pillow for you. Just to lay your head on.

Guy x

Guy Pearce: musician, filmmaker, internationally renowned Australian actor

19

Dear Mum

I am just seeking some clarification re: the boundless love and affection that you have given me over the years.

Recently I was told by a complete stranger that I had a face only a mother could love, and it got me thinking, 'I wonder if you only love me because you're my mum?' So I just wanted to 'unpack' this statement a little, or should I say … do a 'deep dive' into this theory.

Firstly, what kind of face would you want a child to have if you had a choice, and if you could change my face, what would you change? In many ways I hope you're happy enough with the face I've got, because it's hard not to notice that you made my big brother Clayton's face pretty much exactly the same as mine, albeit a bit older.

You made the faces of my dear sisters, Kim and Nat, much different from us boys, which I think was a very good idea. So well done there.

The love you offered was seemingly limitless and endless to us all growing up, and it is still the case now that all your four babies are fully grown adults with babies of our own. Now your grandchildren are receiving the same wholesale quantities of love from you. (PS I hope you're happy with their faces.)

On reflection though, there were a few moments when it could be argued that even being my mum may not have been enough for you to act with unconditional love.

Such as when you drove the family Morris 1800 with me and some of my mates in it onto the school oval and did a doughnut in full view of the kids at school in an attempt to embarrass me, and possibly get me in trouble with the teachers as well. Then, after dropping me off, as you drove away you yelled out of the car window, 'I love you Shaney Waney' at the top of your voice for all to hear, which completely undid all the coolness of your previous circle work on the oval.

There was also the time I said I was going to leave home at the age of about five because you wouldn't give me some lollies. So you helped me pack some clothes and a ham sandwich into a towel, which we tied to a stick and I walked up to the very end of our seemingly very long street with said care package over my shoulder, just like my favourite book character at the time, Tom Sawyer. On reaching the end of the street, I turned around and came straight back home, and sat down at the kitchen table to eat my ham sandwich. You poured me a glass of milk and said, 'Welcome back.' But I guess even in those moments, you offered me love and support.

You did your best to teach me all that I would need to know to survive a grown-up world. Such as when you sat me on the end of my bed and said, 'Now darling, it's time we talked about the birds and the bees', to which I replied, 'Mum, I think I'm a bit too young for this.' And you said, 'Fair enough, let me know when you're ready.' We never really did get to have that chat, but it turns out it wasn't all that necessary, because the truth is, I have never seen a bird have sex with a bee, so it looks like I never really needed to understand it.

Bravery was also something that you had an unlimited supply of. I wonder if this too is something only a mother can have. You gave birth to the four of us, and said that it was wonderful. You had two brain haemorrhages and never once complained. You did the discs in your spine and slept on our billiard table for a while and made out that was all fine. I have watched you say goodbye to all of your seven brothers and sisters and most of their wives and husbands, and yet you still describe your life as blessed. And now you have had Parkinson's for over eighteen years and still have a smile on your face that lights up a room. Yet whenever I got as much as a paper cut, I wanted to tell you how much it hurt so you could comfort me and tell me it was going to be okay.

Well, I have tried to be a little like you Mum, and also tried to surround myself with people like you. I found a wife who is as loving and as kind as you. I have children who have a heart like yours. I have friends who are right by my side just like you. And then I thought, what if everyone was like you, then the world would be a better place, but the world can't be like you, because you're one of a kind, and my favourite bit is … you're mine.

Love your son

Shane

Shane Jacobson: AFI Award-winning actor–writer, presenter, entertainer, author, director, producer and motorsport enthusiast

Dear Mum

Sorry I haven't written to you for a while ... I feel a bit bad about that actually.

I remember clearly when we first started writing to each other regularly ... every week actually ... when I went to Rathkeale boarding school in Masterton at the age of twelve.

I used to look forward to the mail arriving in the common room each morning ... and the prefects handing out the letters and little parcels. As soon as I saw your beautiful handwriting and my name ... my heart sang ... as I knew I was in for some loving life lessons from you ... and some difficult long-division maths from Dad.

I missed you soooo much then ... almost as much as I miss you now ... but at least back in the '60s I knew I'd be seeing you during the school holidays ... or on the next exeat weekend ... now all I have are my memories, the photos ... and your letters. I kept every one of them ... as you did mine! I've put them all together ...

Mum … I think of you every day … especially today … your birthday!

You would have been 96 today!

Happy birthday.

There are so many wonderful things I would have loved to have shared with you over the past 21 years.

I know you weren't exactly thrilled when I decided to move to another country … but you always enjoyed coming to Sydney for another adventure … and I always loved going 'home' to see you and Dad.

What a night it was when we attended the event at Circular Quay … when 'the winner is Syd-a-ney' was announced. You said … as we walked past the Opera House with a million others from the overseas passenger terminal … 'Why would you want to live anywhere else Rich …? This is the place for you.'

I miss your visits … I would have loved you to have been there when I was awarded the Order of Australia. The governor said some really nice things about me … I thought of you throughout the entire ceremony.

Mum … you'd be so proud of the family you created.

Pip and her balding hubby, Murray, are fantastic … and their three beautiful daughters are all safe, well married … and producing magnificent offspring with enthusiasm.

My strongest memory of you and Adam … well, apart from the day I told you and Dad that I was going to be a father and get married at the age of eighteen … was when you and I went to Whanganui for his twenty-first birthday back in 1994. You'll be happy to know he still has the cleanest and tidiest bedroom in the whole of the North Island, is in rude health, performs the haka at least a dozen times a day ... and still has the rug you gave him on his bedroom floor.

I don't see him enough ... it's hard at the mo ... I need to fix that when I can.

Becky continues to do everything perfectly ... as well as you two sharing initials and a second name ... Frances ... there is a lot of you in her! She's grown into a superb woman ... is having a brilliant career ... and she and James are expecting a little sister for Bella early next year! I'm pushing for them to call her Romola ... but don't hold your breath for that! (Oops ... too soon?)

Nick is awesome ... he's also excelling in his career ... making TV shows the whole country watches. He continues his uncanny knack of being able to fix anything and assemble stuff with a sixth sense! He's such a solid, strong, decent person ... reminds me so much of your hubby/my dad. People always say ... 'If you're putting a team together ... Nick is always everyone's first pick!'

Christian ... well, you only met him briefly when he was little. You made each other giggle. He's also grown into a fine young man ... blessed with charm, wit, talent and personality plus!

Like all your grandchildren he has a deep intellect ... and a passion to do things his way! You did that when you went to university in your youth ... he chose not to do that ... and is sailing uncharted waters ... making his unique mark ... setting the stage for a colourful life.

Estella ... well ... you didn't see her coming!!! She turned sixteen last month ... and, like you ... adores horses ... they are pretty much her life! She rides every week ... and like you did, she goes to a great boarding school where she is loved and nurtured. She also ... like all my beautiful children ... bears the RFW signature trademark ... the hands you inherited from Papa ... the chunky sausage fingers etc. ... you know the ones! Her mum ... who boasts magnificent seamstresses' fingers took a while to get used to that! Ha! ... All good now!

You'd adore each one of them as they would you ...

Mum ... not a day goes by when I don't think of you ... and I often quote you ... 'As my mum would say ... there are two ways to do anything ... the easy way ... and the right way!' ... or 'If you're going somewhere ... take something' ... and my personal favourite ... 'If you always tell the truth ... you never have to remember anything!'

I'm glad I was prompted to write this letter to you by my friend Samuel Johnson ... he's a great guy ... and YOU ... by any standards, were a great mum.

I know everyone adores their mothers ... as indeed they should ... but I know for a fact that I had 'One for the Ages'.

Miss you

Rich xx

PS I've put in my will ... that half my ashes be scattered at Balmoral Beach ... followed by a big party ... and that the other half join you and Dad on that beautiful, sunny hillside in Katikati. x

Richard Wilkins AM: presenter, host, entertainment editor, bestselling author

Dear Mum

God knows the crap that came your way every year. Coasters for the coffees you never drank. Rigatoni jewellery. A soldier made of pipe-cleaners. Every year, like hard-rubbish day in reverse, the DIY knick-knacks piled up, the collages and finger paintings, the misshapen mugs, the pinewood savoury dish nobody trusted.

Of course, if anything saved my bacon it was the cards. Remember them? The corny poems and acrostics. Maybe you keep a stash somewhere. If anything, the cards were the presents with assorted bits of trash attached. Say what you like about my needlework, but at least I could embroider a sentence. Big thanks to you, Heather Astle – your love of words a fire blazing in me still.

Hence I've skipped the macramé. No charcoal unicorn this time round. Instead, I've gone straight for the message, spelling out my gratitude the old-school way. That's right, just a card this time, a letter-game to bung on your mini-fridge.

THANK YOU Mum. T-H-A-N-K Y-O-U. Please excuse the absence of papier-mâché frog.

TUBA – Skinny kids got the clarinets, and big boys the brass. My albatross was the tuba. Worse than heavy, it was cumbersome. A brown suitcase with swollen sides, like trying to carry a walrus down the street. To this day, I still can't read music, but that didn't stop me from playing in the Frenchs Forest Primary School Orchestra, oomping and parping when the baton pointed my way, just as I laboured the valves at home, making the whole family suffer. Nonetheless, there you were, come the brunt of summer, the passenger door unlocked, or when it rained, your umbrella sprung open at the school gate, ready to chauffeur that walrus home.

HOW-TO – Too many to count, your invisible lessons. Like how to read, and keep reading, getting lost in a novel long after it was done. How to care; how to swim; how to say turmeric. How to avoid absolutes because they can always be disproven, and by always, I mean usually. How to small-talk and think big. But most of all how to unravel a cryptic clue. Now look what you started.

ASTRONAUT – Before Neil Armstrong walked the moon, I travelled outer space in my Balgowlah rocket. The cockpit was the nose-cone, often tricky to reach. Some days, the stars felt closer compared to climbing that iron ladder. Five levels high, a skeleton rocket cemented on Dobroyd Head, where you held your ground to encourage me. Parking the pram near the sand, you gave me wings, spurred me to wriggle upwards, from base to helm where other kids might be in charge. Bigger kids. Aliens. Yet nothing so terrifying as to keep me from climbing, not with you as Ground Control, less the helicopter than a launchpad mum, the start of my every adventure as I clambered through the hatchways, from one storey to the next, the blood-perfume of the metal, the growing sprawl of light, as the top gave way to the harbour, the shrunken earth, that duco-blue ozone. And from there to Andromeda.

NERINGAH – They called it recycling. Not tins and bottles, but mothers, women stranded mid-career thanks to kids popping up. Before the wedding ring and teething rusks, you were a professional. The first wave of occupational therapists, you'd helped people use their bodies again, to balance on stairs and open a tin of peaches. Until motherhood interrupted. Until you and I became inseparable, going to beaches and chatting, your life usurped by children and other mothers. Ten years on, both of us older, your head was turned by talk of recycling, getting back into caring on a grander scale, and you took it. Refreshing your degree, you found a parallel universe in Neringah, lending strategy to its brittle residents. Loving them. Cheering them to independence in your slacks and lanyard, those daggy party hats you forgot to remove between rehab and supermarket. Back then, as a teen, I thought you were being selfish, leaving us to manage our afternoons, but you were being the opposite, living against the grain, helping us find independence too. Neringah was a word, a world, to deepen us all.

KNOCK-KNOCK – Who's there? Heather. Heather who? Heather last of David's knock-knocks and riddles and pop songs and stories and anagrams? Sorry. You never did. I was relentless. I was the torrent to your rock, neither of us capitulating. Every day, from A to Z, from lame jokes to timid essays, you copped it, my outpouring to your audience.

YABBIES – Two kinds. The mud-coloured monsters that hid in the Dural dam, your family farm where nursery labels hung from giant trees, like toe-tags stuck on the living. And the see-through yabbies we sucked from sand, working the plunger along the lagoon's edge. Two sacred places, haunted by yabbies, both totems outraged by the sudden air. Wendover and Ku-ring-gai – two vivid realms that still gnaw my imagination, indelible places hidden down tracks you knew by heart.

ONIONSKIN – The plan was simple. Every month, like clockwork, I'd send you an envelope filled with brainteasers, small puzzles I'd make in transit, tracing the Andes, or waiting for socks to dry in Munich. (Aside from garfish, how many animals can you list with GAR in their names? That's an example, plus 23 other Wordwit puzzles every month, always on onionskin to lessen the cost, each one scheduled to run in the *Herald* – my cash cow.) But I needed you in between, my typist and decoder, my midwife and attorney, my proofreader and accomplice. In short, my mum. I paid you in updates and imprecisions. I paid you nothing. Without you Lee Starheath, your working alias, the Andes may as well have been on the moon.

UNDERTOW – I'm lying face-up in the wash, the waves too small to bother with. I might be eight or nine, a boy on the brink of being older. The family umbrella is planted near the baths where the girls want to swim. You can't be everywhere, after all. Mind this, I'd said, plunking the surf mat by your towel and bolting for the water. So strong, the current knocked my ankles sideways. Instead of resisting, I let the force sweep me. A star in silhouette, I lay on my back, the noise of the beach lost in my heartbeat. The clouds moved, or I moved under them. The rip was streaming north to south, away from the baths and heading for Manly. Another boy would panic. A smarter kid would never think himself safe in this situation. But I could swim, thanks to you. I was buoyant, thanks to you, my anchor under the green umbrella. Arms splayed, eyes to the sky, as if to prove these things were true, I let the current have its way, your son in the lap of the ocean, calm, ecstatic.

Love

David

David Astle: full-time word nerd, crossword maker, Wordplay *columnist, broadcaster, author and co-host of SBS cult show* Letters and Numbers

Dear Mum

Once when you were asked what the Tongan word is for 'silence woman!' you replied, 'There is none, end the story!' What a great answer. Typically, short not sweet. Direct and empowering just like you. But we did always wonder if this were a little white lie? You are a natural born leader and have always spoken with such conviction that whatever you have said to us we have taken to be the gospel truth.

You've recently started saying 'Google it, I'm right!' just to prove to us that even the internet can't beat you. The thing is we do google it behind your back, and you are always right goddammit. Except for that one time – we looked up 'silence woman' in the English to Tongan translator and there it was in black and white: '*longo, fefine*'. You cheeky devil! Thank you for keeping this from the men in the house. You're a quick thinker!

English is not your first language but you haven't let it stop you from spelling it out better than anyone we know. Okay, sometimes you get your plurals and genders mixed up but that's about it. After all, who in their right mind would correct you when you say things like 'Why are mens talking?' Certainly not Dad. Over the years he's learnt the hard way. Once when he saw a pretty lady and mistakenly said out loud 'Oh she's a pretty little sheila', your comeback was 'Oh yeah, and what you going to do with it?' In your opinion 'all mens are the same', even our well-meaning father.

Lately you've taken to texting and FaceTime. You are pretty good on the emojis too. We've noticed that you have your favourites. Usually a single love heart then prayer hands followed by the laughing face, but recently you've expanded your repertoire to include the looney face. Do you think we're mad? Is this a mistake? Maybe you need to power up your spectacle prescription because you've made some other classic typos lately. Did you really mean to say 'good luck, knock them deaf' before our recent live performance on national television? Because it really threw us. Made worse by Dad's recommendation to 'remember to sing not shout'. You more than made up for it afterwards with your follow-up text: 'My jolly goodness, that was absolutely topped everything! Interview was short. Sweet! So so very proud and good on you both. Well deserve and can't wait for next chapter. Bless everyone souls whoever they are. Congratulations millions time. Very proud, very stoke.'

Thank you for not taking a step back and for embracing technology at 86 years old.

We love you Mum you naughty funny woman.

Vika and Linda

Vika and Linda Bull: singing sisters, Music Victoria Hall of Fame inductees

Dear Mum

My Darling Mum, Hey Rosie,

How do I start a letter to the most important person in my life, and what do I want to say?

I want to say you're my first memory, and that memory is unbridled attachment. I would be four or five years old and trying to imagine a life without you and all I saw was an empty night sky in my mind.

Then as I got older and my enthusiastic, exuberant personality evolved, you embraced it unconditionally. You let me feel totally confident in being 'me', and that if someone thought I was 'too loud, too hyperactive, too dreamy' that it was really their problem. I was a free spirit and you embraced it, totally.

But you also encouraged me to be observant, curious, to nurture my friendships and, most of all, to go after my dream.

I love your laugh, your historical and political knowledge, your passion for music and the arts, your freedom of expression (and yes, swearing) and your love for us, your kids and grandkids. But God help ANYBODY who calls you Grandma.

When I was pregnant with my daughter, all I wanted was to wear an oversized red wool cardigan that I remember you wearing when I was little. I felt so safe, and also a huge sense of love and comfort when I wore it. That's my overriding memory of you Mum. Love, humour, music, colour, acceptance, vigorous debates, shouting at the TV, long conversations and a huge smile.

Love from

George

Georgie Parker: acclaimed Australian actor (All Saints, Home and Away)

Dear Mum

I haven't gone mad. I know you died three years ago but I miss you, and Samuel Johnson suggested I write a letter. It actually seems much longer since we lost you because the ravages of dementia stole you away long before your frail body took its last breath. Speaking of which, the euthanasia debate is starting again in South Australia and I hope it will get up because there are many people who would not choose to end their life in pain, misery or, as in your case, profound and fearful confusion and emptiness.

On a happier note, Dad lived on in his hilarious and merry way sucking the marrow out of every day. We all thought he would be a bit hopeless after you left, but despite you completely spoiling him (and us) every day, he must have picked up a few tricks along the way. At least he could no longer blame you if his steak was overdone. His alternate-day diet of fillet steak then salmon (with the constant of a salad and a couple or three glasses of white wine) was pretty much only interrupted if he came to one of our places for tea. And we usually gave him a steak then anyway. And every night he set the table for brekky and put his milk in a little jug just like you did. I think those rituals helped keep you close for him. Without you there to remind him with your discreet signal, he sometimes sat with one of his testicles popping out the bottom of his shorts. But that just made us laugh and think of you.

It would be nice to know that you guys have hooked up again after Dad died two years ago. That was all a bit of a saga! You might know I'm kind of a big deal now! Those scallywag kids in Thailand got stuck in a cave and I headed over there to help out with the rescue. See, I told you guys that all those years of cave diving would pay off! Anyway, everyone was pretty pleased with us and we ended up meeting the governor-general and the prime minister. But what you'll be most excited to hear is that we even met a couple of the royals, Harry and Meghan! I remember as a kid, if the queen or one of them would appear on the telly, we'd all shout out 'ROYALS!' and you'd come running in from the kitchen to watch. We still sometimes do that at home even though you aren't there. I wish I could have told you all about it in person. Of course, Dad died on the last day of the cave rescue, about the time the last kid came out alive. Actually, I seem to recall you hung on until the queen's birthday. Maybe you do get to choose your time.

I miss you both, look after the old fella wherever you both are and please, do not write back. I would find that somewhat disturbing.

Lots of love

Bert xo

PS Did you get the copy of the *Woman's Day* we put in Dad's coffin? It had a picture of me AND some royals on the cover! *Richard Harris SC OAM: cave diver, author, 2019 Australian of the Year, Star of Courage recipient for heroic involvement in the 2019 Thai cave rescue*

Dear Mum

When Samuel asked if I wanted to write a letter to my mother to be published in a book, I wondered what I could say to you that I haven't already said in person.

Are there things I need you to know before it's too late? I'm not saying that in a fatalistic, end of the world kind of way but more because the last few years have really shown that we don't know what is around the corner and it's vital that we share our thoughts/love/stories/regrets/forgiveness before it's too late and we are gone. I would hate to leave this earth with people not knowing I loved them and that if they had done anything to hurt me that I also forgive them as I hope I will be forgiven for the damage I have done to others. I truly believe that it is by holding on to the pain of the past we can never fully grow to be the people we were born to be, and it's you who taught me that. Forgiveness was something I struggled with in my early life, particularly my teens and 20s. Not the everyday whoops sorry I broke that glass, told a white lie, said you were fat and called you really mean things kind of forgiveness. Somehow those stuff-ups were the easiest to forgive. We did it all the time. As a family we witnessed the abuse and the 'I'm sorry' and the 'don't worry about it, let's just move on' on a daily basis. In a way it made it easy for us to forgive others for mild slights, even biggish ones. Holding a grudge was never really in my psyche.

Except for Grandad. That was a biggie. How do you forgive someone who has done so much damage to not only you but to the people closest to you? The person closest to you. Your mother. But I needed to only look at you to see how it was done. How you continuously forgave Grandad and then Dad for the countless hours, days, weeks, months and years of suffering they both inflicted on you. I'm not going to go into the morbid details. A Google search will sort that out for anyone who wants to know, but what I will say is that it is because of you and your ability to always see the good in others that I am the person I am today. Your capacity to leave behind the painful wounds of the past and to look to a future with positivity and optimism has been the greatest gift you could give me.

I am the glass half full kind of girl. I do believe life will get better. Sometimes you get lemons but you make lemonade. And when the days come that are bad and you feel like shit then you have a damn good howl, let it all out and know that there is a way out. Even when you feel like you are in a pit as I did. And you know it was a deep one. But through it all there was always two words that kept coming back to me. Two words that saved my life.

Surrender and faith.

Surrender your pain, your fear, your guilt and your shame. Surrender to the small still voice inside that is listening and that will forgive you and love you and nurse you back from the brink. Let it out and let it go. You are loved and you are safe.

And faith. Faith that there IS a greater good. That we are being cared for by a power, source, energy far greater than we can ever fathom. Some call that God or a higher power. Some believe it's our inner wisdom or our instinct. I know what it means to me and that's all that matters. That feeling has always been with me because you gave it to me Mum. You always made me feel loved no matter what. Cherished no matter what. Forgiven no matter what. I believe in God's love because you showed it to me first.

Surrender, forgiveness, faith and love. Lessons from my mum, Shirley. I love the fact that I have been given the opportunity to let other people know a little more about you, and maybe someone will read something in these words and that will help them overcome something in their life because you are the reason I overcame some of the biggest tests in mine. I know I say it to you at the end of every telephone call Mum, but I hope that this letter will simply reinforce how very loved you are. How cherished you are. How blessed I am to have been able to call you my mother. The best human I know. The best parent. The only one I ever needed. Thank you will never be enough ...

R

Rebecca Gibney: multi-Logie and AFI Award-winning actor
(Halifax, Packed to the Rafters)

Dear Mum

Hadassah. I prefer to use your name. I want people to know you were far more than a loyal mother. You were a woman of many unsung talents, hard-won skills. A seamstress: trained in the workshops of Bialystok. Eastern Poland. Border country. Disputed territory. 'Seamstress' sells you short. You possessed the skills of a tailor; you designed and made your own clothes.

You were a singer too. Your repertoire of Yiddish songs was vast. Before the war you performed at community gatherings. You loved your life in Bialystok, the comradeship, the sense of purpose. You were fired up by ideals for a better world. Yet it ended badly. You got out just in time, but you lost your entire family, bar two sisters, to genocide. Post-war, your singing was confined to a single-fronted terrace in Canning Street, Carlton North, located in a neighbourhood of immigrants creating a new life.

You sang for hours on end as you went about your chores. Your mezzo-soprano rang strong. But there was an edge to your singing. You were possessed by ghosts. The loss of your family, community, had shattered your youthful beliefs. You felt that life had betrayed you. But you never lost your faith in music. Yiddish was the mother tongue. English your sixth language. And you picked it up quickly. I see you at the kitchen table, preparing the evening meal, singing. 'When Irish Eyes Are Smiling'. 'Where have you been, Billy Boy, Billy Boy?'. Songs you picked up from the radio.

Yes, there were times when you raged at the loss. But in later years, there were also periods of reverie. Your job was done. You had brought up your three sons. You had endured. There was a gentler tone to the singing. As an author, I have written about both the rage and the reverie. But it is your reverie that I return to these days – the picture of you, in your final year, seated at the kitchen table. Gazing at a window, located high up on the opposite wall.

The window was divided into twelve squares, framing the upper branches of a tree. In winter the branches were bare. In spring they were clothed in green. In the twilight stillness, you could hear the twitter of birds. 'Birds can speak,' you once said. 'They have a language of their own. They probably talk about where they have been for the past year. They perch on that tree and chatter to each other. You can hear how pleased they are to be back.' This was your seventh language. The most comforting, and musical, of all.

Love you Hadassah.

Always will.

Arnold Zable: award-winning writer, storyteller, educator and human rights advocate

Dear Mum

I'm sorry you never got the chance to meet your mum – your biological mum. What a bloody surprise it was to find out you were adopted! And there we were thinking we had the long-life genes of the parents who brought you up.

You have been on such an epic journey to find out where you came from – with all the surprises, excitement and deep sadness along the way.

I just wish we could have found her. I just wish we knew what happened. It is a terrific mystery. She walked out of that hospital in Perth after giving birth to you, and disappeared. No death record. No marriage record. No record of her leaving the country. No census record. No trace.

It's almost as if she never existed at all – like she was a ghost.

But she is alive in you. In me. In us.

And you got to meet your brother, just briefly before he passed away from cancer. You were not an only child after all. I still CAN NOT believe that my DNA test resulted in us finding him just weeks before he died. It was some kind of miracle. You got to tell him all about the mum you guys shared, all the facts that you knew, all the photographs that you had found over the years of researching. If only you guys had had more time.

Maybe one day we will find out what happened to her, your mum, Eileen. I hope so. I hope she ended up having a happy life.

I've loved sharing this journey, and I am incredibly proud of you – my 100 per cent Irish mum.

Love

Favel

Favel Parrett: author, Miles Franklin Literary Award shortlistee, surfer, dingo devotee

Dear Mum

You were just eighteen when you came on the boat from Italy. No family, no contacts, no English. Fronting up to a canning factory with the question Dad helped you learn: 'Have you got a job for me?' Then to the country to run a pub – a universe away from your old life. You've lived such an adventure. Always fierce, never a backward step.

With four boys, there wasn't room for easy words. But I felt it all the same – in the froth you shared from your coffee, the pancakes on Saturdays, and the rice soup when I was sick.

I remember something Toni Morrison wrote: 'Grown don't mean nothing to a mother. A child is a child. They get bigger, older, but grown? What's that supposed to mean? In my heart it don't mean a thing.'

Same for you, I think.

Then, these past few years, we watched you care for Dad. Your heart was breaking, but you never failed him. He couldn't have wished for more, and we couldn't either.

Because even when you call me *scemo* (idiot), *barbone* (vagrant), or *stupido* (self-explanatory), I know what you really mean.

And I love you too, Mum.

Mark x

Mark Brandi: runner and award-winning writer

Dear Mum

You are so many parts of me. I'm caring and ruthless in equal measure. You would sit on my bed singing me hymns during those long agonising nights when I had inner-ear abscesses throbbing inside my eight-year-old head, *Gather round the table of the lord, eat his body, drink his blood and we'll sing a song of love allelu allelu alleluia.* I loved those hymns. *Brother, sister we are one and our lives have just begun in the spirit we are young and we'll live forever.* They made me feel like I was a bit invincible, like God was on our side, like you'd summoned him into my corner. It helped, I slept until the abscesses burst and I went into a delirium. Then it was off to hospital, poisoned from the goo. You were so gentle and loving it made me want to be tender. But you were tough in the clinches Mum. I guess Mum if your mum dies when you're twelve, you grow up during the war, migrate in your 20s, have three children and your husband dies when you're 55 – you'll toughen.

I've never seen anybody so coldly and clinically scythe off a friendship for a perceived misstep. I've also got a bit of that female lion, instinctive and brutal when it comes to the brood. Ruthless.

And then there's the many philosophies or truisms I find myself whispering out loud to myself or saying to my own girls. Make the bed and the whole house looks clean. Put a hat on and keep your feet warm. You can run away with a bag of money but you can't get far with a bag of clothes. People make a party – if you're invited, turn up. Bugger what people think. Lawrence, have you forgiven yourself lately?

That was always a big one for me, out of the blue many times throughout my life you'd ask that massive question – 'Have you forgiven yourself lately?' – and it had the same effect as the hymns. You made me feel worthy and strong.

I love you Mum

Loz xx

Lawrence Mooney: award-winning stand-up comedian, radio broadcaster, television host

Dear Mum

My father thinks I'm an absolute angel but you, as a realist, know that I'm not.

I'll start by apologising for my behaviour over the years. There have been many incidents, but I am pretty sorry that you had to pick me up from the police station not once, but twice, when I was thirteen. That was rather embarrassing for you, I do understand that now as a mother.

I spent a lot of time grounded when I was a teenager, and I'm not going to thank you for that! But something you said to me quite a few times during those years – and it's always stayed with me – is this: 'It's called karma, and when you have your own kids it'll come back to bite you.' As always, you were right. But I got through everything with my boys with your support.

One thing that really stands out to me is how much you helped me when I first fell pregnant. Nineteen, pregnant and about to be kicked out of the army … not on your watch! You made sure that I came home, had the baby, had my son sleeping all night at six weeks of age and supported me through all of that. Going through that and then going back into a military career at all of nineteen was really quite difficult, so I'll always be grateful that you were beside me.

In the toughest times of my life, you have always been there for me. When I went through my battle with Veterans' Affairs, there were times when we weren't talking, but you were still looking after me.

You also supported me when I was trying to get my Senate seat the first time round – you made it very clear you thought I was never going to make it, but you pretended that you did! I appreciated that.

I know it takes a lot to upset you, but I can still remember the look in your eyes when I came home after I lost my Senate seat. It almost broke me.

Writing this letter I'm thinking a lot about my childhood, record player and 200 records we used to have. You were really good about letting me have my friends over all the time to hang out and listen to them. We might have been living in housing commission, but they were probably some of the best memories of my life.

You've always been the disciplinarian, and while I never showed it, I'm very grateful for that. You still have no problem telling me what to do, even though I'm almost 50 ... although I probably still need it!

Thanks for being my mum.

Jacqui

Jacqui Lambie: former Australian Defence Force soldier, Tasmanian senator

Dear Mum

I was going to ring you the other day and then I remembered that I couldn't. It still feels like you are here with me and I am sure you are. I don't need to call you because I know you can still hear me.

You are not missing much. I think you are much better off up there with Dad and most of your family. Don't worry about us. You enjoy yourself in heaven. You have earned happiness.

I remember when I was a little kid, probably about five. The Vietnam War was on and there were lots of ads on TV advertising the army. I thought to myself, 'Yep, I want to join the army.'

I told Chris about it, and he laughed saying that I'd have to be eighteen to join the army. I was not happy with this answer and took my question to Dad, who agreed with Chris that I needed to be eighteen to join the army.

Frustrated I came to you. Your response was exactly what I wanted to hear – 'Well, you never know, they might need someone small like you who could sneak up on people. Why don't we write them a letter and find out.'

So we wrote a letter to the army advising them of my availability. I was happy!

It was a masterful piece of parenting. You heard my problem. Took it seriously and gave me hope. I think I forgot about the whole thing shortly after and never worried about the army's response.

The point being that you fixed my problem, gave me hope and taught me that anything could be possible.

I remember when our train broke down in Kalgoorlie on the way to Perth. The only food available were cold pies. I remember you telling us what an adventure it would be to eat cold pies. Chris and I fell for it hook, line and sinker and were very excited to be eating a cold pie. It was a credit to you that you turned something that was shit into a fun adventure. Once again, it was a great lesson in optimism.

I could go on for hours about all the great times and lessons you taught us but I think your ability to find a silver lining and hope were probably the most important.

Thank you Gug! I will see you in my dreams until we are together again.

All my love

Brian

PS Say hi to Spencer Tracy for me!
Brian Mannix: actor, author, radio presenter, Dancing with the Stars *contestant, energetic frontman of 80's band Uncanny X-Men, winner of Mr Ocean Grove 1971*

Dear Mum

I'm about to lose this game of Words With Friends. I have three tiles left; you have an 80-point lead.

The first sign of my doom was your early-game score of AMPHORAL. I'd scrambled to keep pace (BLUNTED, SNICKER), until, mid-game, I was dealt two consecutive all-vowel racks. 'Gah,' I said to my partner, swiping the app away. 'I'm done for.' Your eye for opportunity, your nose for discovering obscure words – our games are already down-to-the-wire, but this all-vowel setback? Fatal.

According to our stats, we've played 496 games together. You've won 259 games and I've won 237. Your average move score is 31 against my 29.

These tiles are the most words that we exchange nowadays, but we were never great conversationalists to begin with, even when we lived together. We don't use the in-game chat, though we did try in our early days of playing (*you're very good*, you typed once, and another time when I hadn't made a move in 48 hours, *is everything ok*, and another time when I sent a move after midnight, *why are you up so late?*).

When I spend time around other families, I'm startled by how much they talk, how often they hug or say *I love you*. Whenever the mother tries to include me, my instinct is to fold myself away. One time, I went to lunch with an aunt, who chatted and chatted at me while I sank in my seat and missed you with all my heart. I am an animal that can only trust the scent of her mother.

You win the game 457 to 382. I hit REMATCH. The bright circles of our avatars bump together joyously – the tiles are dealt – and I cast the first word.

Elizabeth

Elizabeth Tan: award-winning author

Dear Mum

Letters were a way for you to see the world beyond your blindness.

From an early age I read to you, my own bedtime stories and nursery rhymes, instructions on the bottle of Tame to rid me of my tangles, school homework or teachers' reports, doctors' scripts, even the phone ledger (names for party lists, numbers for calls) and flour packets, plain or self-raising. Then I read your personal and business mail to you, leaving correspondence from close friends till last as a treat. The interpretation of handwritten scripts was not always an easy task to decipher. 'Keep the stamps. Throw it. Pay it. File it. Don't have an opinion. Obey.' Later I read your manuscripts over and over and over again to you, editing the punctuation, grammar, spelling. The carbon paper was in back to front. Fingers were on the wrong keys for a whole page.

Charged with emotion, the first letter I ever wrote to you was from that cold-hearted retreat with the nuns in an icy England seaside town. I was four. Gloomy composure resulting from the whole devastatingly cold experience manifested itself in my desperate sense of hope derived from a postage stamp, despatched to us singularly on a Sunday after mass.

Graduating on to reading your letters to me, I was alone, life had distanced us physically. The thud in the letterbox, sometimes twenty pages of your thoughts, engagements and interludes with people, windows into your world. The care packs of books you sent me over several decades of linguistic exile in Spain, kept my reading alive, relevant, contemporary and in English.

Letter writing became a habit, a hobby, an addiction almost. A connection with the distant homeland, it was a bridge slow to cross with a reliably capricious and untrustworthy delivery service at home in Spain. My own letters to you were always read aloud by someone who inevitably shared any intimacy that was enfolded into their depths.

The letter for you was a document, leading to the publication of a book of lifelong correspondence with my godmother, Judith Wright, and to that famous Collection of Manuscripts by Australian Writers which toured libraries nationally. Brava, brava, brava Barbara.

We now have nothing to say in letters or too much to say to bother writing it all down.

There are no more letters between us.

With love from your one and only daughter

Christabel

Christabel Blackman: visual artist, fine arts conservator, daughter of Charles and Barbara Blackman

Dear Mum

Memories fade over thirty years
the sound of your voice becomes lost in the din
the light in your eyes when you smiled grows dim
and the precise expressions of praise and love, difficult to
    recall.
Thankfully, beyond sound, image and word, lies feeling
So I close my eyes and you are here
as near as my next heartbeat.

*Graeme Connors: songwriter, recording artist, son of Eileen
Connors*

Dear Mum

When Samuel asked me to be a part of this project I jumped at the chance and thought this will be easy and I'd love the opportunity to tell the world how I feel about you.

You are amazing and incredible and fierce and fabulous and explaining that on paper would be a breeze.

But Mum, this has actually been the toughest thing I've ever written because the reality is there are no words to adequately describe you, and not enough words in the English language to thank you for being my mum.

Yes, you are awesome, but so is a nice holiday, so that word doesn't work; yes, you are amazing, but so is a great dinner, so that word isn't enough either; yes, you are incredible, but then so was the first moon landing, and you are a trillion times more impressive than that.

So I can't find the words to thank you or praise you enough for being the world's best mum, a guiding light, a stabilising force in any storm, an ever-positive beam of light sent straight from the heavens above.

You always have been and always will be a massive part of my life, except when I was hosting *Celebrity Dog School* and you momentarily disowned me, but I'm glad we got through that.

Lots of love Mum from

The world's oldest Mummy's Boy xxxx

Larry Emdur: host of The Morning Show *and* Weekend Sunrise, *and former host of everything that's ever been aired on Australian television (including* The Price is Right)

Dear Mum

It's been so long since we said goodbye to you, I thought my heart would break and I wouldn't be able to go on, but life does go on and you just learn to live with it. I realised I would never lose you as you would always be a huge part of me and my life.

You're always a great inspiration to me because you found the good in everyone. Being one of ten children and losing your father at three you had a struggle from the beginning of life. Luckily you loved your mum and your brothers and sisters, and you all looked out for each other. I miss them too.

Because you had a wonderful life with Dad and you miscarried many times, I've always felt so lucky to be the child that survived and became the bonus to your beautiful marriage. We lost Dad far too early, at 53, and I know he was the love of your life.

He was such a good man. I remember so well when you had your car accident after dropping me to GTV9 when I was sixteen. They thought you would be in a wheelchair and never walk again. Dad was by your side every minute, and after six months in the Alfred Hospital you proved them all wrong and started to walk. He did everything for you, looked after you and treated you like a queen. I guess you thought your life would end when he died suddenly, but you were so strong. As I was overseas, Bert made a promise to him that he would always look after you and me. And he did. We got married that year, 1974, and your new life began.

Our two children were the love of your life and you spent a lot of time with both Matthew and Lauren. You came on every holiday with us, and when going overseas, you said that you took Dad with you every time, because it was a dream of his.

Sometimes I do get really sad when I think of how much you loved family life and how much you are missing now. We've had lots of ups and downs over the years, but like you I'm so lucky to be such a happy person and focus on the positives. A wonderful husband, great kids and now six fabulous grandchildren, Mum – you would adore them, I think Lauren did the job for you with babies.

They are just such a delight. Sam Albert, Eva Eunice, Lola Patricia, Monty Matthew, Perla Dolly and Alby James. Lauren and Matt, her husband, are wonderful parents and she loves being a mum. Bert and I are so lucky we live close to them and see the kids every day.

The thing I get sad about is knowing how you would love to be making dolls' clothes with them and teaching them songs like you did with Matthew and Lauren.

Sometimes I think of the things you did for me, like making all my clothes and taking me to dancing school and *Swallow's*

Juniors. I hope you knew how much I appreciated it and how much I loved you for it.

I know money was always tight but I don't think I ever wanted for anything. I'd go to school and would come home to find an outfit you had made for me during the day or even a new bedspread. You were so clever. You know I still have some of the hand-beaded dresses that you made me for TV, I just can't part with them.

I'm now 75 and I feel more like you every day. I love my friends – most of them you know because I've had them since I was very young. And I do and say things just like you did, sometimes not quite right, and everyone says, 'What was that Eun?'

I've said how lucky I am a few times in this letter, but you know, I think it's more than just luck. I had a wonderful life with you and Dad and have always known where I wanted to be and what I wanted to do. You were a great role model, gave good advice, but let me do my own thing.

I hope I'm loved as much as you are.

I miss you but I'll take you with me wherever I go.

Love you

Patti xxx

*Patti Newton AM: Australian showbiz royalty (*In Melbourne Tonight, Good Morning Australia, *3AW)*

Dear Mum

I was going to write you a heartfelt letter to show my gratitude and love for the life you've given me, and after running over the same themes, I stopped to think what would Mum really like ...?

So it came to me.

You've always connected with the sound of my voice (as you've heard it the longest and loudest of anyone) ... some of those times I'm not so proud of (sorry).

Your sunshine has been my light.

You sang to me from the moment I entered the world and you haven't stopped. I'm glad you let your voice out and I don't care if it's in tune or not!!

Thank you for your joy, laughter and sunshine.

I love you eternally. This is your song.

Mother

Mother in the mirror
mother in the aging face
mother is the sunshine
keeper of the goodness safe

Mother of the family
mother of the truth in the dark
mother is the safety
handing out the help when it's hard

It's golden and it's pure
like a fortress so secure
through the ages
till kingdom come
there is nothing
like a mother's love

Mother in the garden
mother digging out the thorns
mother of the cradle
sacred in the birth we're joined

Mother on the horseback
mother in a holy place
mother lifts the burden
stronger than a man can take

It's golden and it's pure
like a fortress so secure
through the ages
till kingdom come

there is nothing
like a mother's love

Mother in the drought
mother in the flooding rain
mother fix the broken
the hungry and the losers' pain

Mother in the moment
mother in the memory
mother in the language
teaching there's more we can be

It's golden and it's pure
like a fortress so secure
through the ages
till kingdom come
there is nothing
like a mother's love
and I thank you
for all you've done

Love you forever

Fliss

Felicity Urquhart: multi-Golden Guitar Award-winning country
singer–songwriter, TV presenter (Bennett, Bowtell & Urquhart)

Dear Mum

There's a photo of you and your dearest friend. You're in your 20s and you're both sporting skirts so outrageously short that it's hard to believe you were allowed to wear them in public. You're both laughing as if you've just heard the best joke ever.

Your friendship was almost new then, and you couldn't know what was ahead. She couldn't know how much she would need you, and how you would always be there when she did. You couldn't know that your friendship would last the rest of a lifetime – hers. Except the bond you shared was stronger than death, because you both worked to make it so.

Such friendships tend to be unique – except you have several of them. Women you've known for over 60 years, some less than that; some of them haven't lived near you for decades and some are down the road. These are friendships tended with care and concern, because you understand that love is best expressed in small ways rather than grand gestures.

This is the most precious work of everyday life, of being human; it is often unacknowledged, sometimes taken for granted. But your children noticed, even if we didn't always say it. From you we learnt how to be friends, with other people and with each other. We learnt that as wonderful as it is to say 'I love you' it is just as important to show it. We will probably never say it and show you enough to express how much we owe you, but we'll keep at it.

Love,

Sophie

Sophie Green: bestselling author, publisher and country music aficionado

Dear Mum

In the wee small hours …

Me:
'Stay. Please stay. Why
can't you stay here? the
full moon above the
ocean so near water and
light we have all we
need … Please stay stay
my dear mother stay
with me here.'

Mum:
'But the world
keeps on turning it
rolls on and on how
can I stay my
tomorrow is gone
in my shadows are

demons waiting to
pounce suck out
my blood take
every ounce of my
spirit, my son, of
loving romance.'

Me:
'then forget, forget, forget
for tonight

Demons can't grab you
in the full of moonlight
no usurer's lackey will
give you a fright we are
alone in our skin, in our
blood, in our breath, in
our love here is no debt
here no regret here is
just us soft and frail
here we are, Mum
where we love in the
moonlight …'

Always your little

Davey-John

*John Howard: Logie Award-winning actor, poet, painter, director
and sometime farmer*

Dear Mum

I wouldn't be doing what I am doing if you weren't the guiding force throughout my life. I was one of those kids who wasn't much good at anything. It was almost like the Gaylord Focker scenario, from *Meet the Fockers*.

Any minor achievement I happened to fluke was a massive triumph for you, my dear mother (along with the long-suffering relatives), to celebrate. Hell! Third in the egg and spoon race – 'Isn't he amazing?'

What this allowed me to do, and become, was extremely important for my later career.

Deep down, I knew I hadn't achieved much at all. However, I did know I wouldn't be admonished for failure – I would only be encouraged to try, because what I had achieved by coming second last in the 50-metre freestyle was astounding, as you convincingly pointed out.

I really didn't fear failure, as I had failed, and was lauded for my efforts – it was all about trying.

You were always frighteningly loyal to me, and most times I was wrong; you would stand by me – a mother's unconditional love.

As you got older I made sure I would do your shopping and have dinner with you at least once a week – we really got on exceedingly well.

I miss you, and think about you so much – before you passed I sat with you and told you how much you had done, and how grateful I was.

I could have gone in many directions, but you encouraged me to travel my road; as you said, 'Destiny chooses one for each of us.'

Russell

Russell Morris AM: singer–songwriter, guitarist and ARIA Hall of Fame inductee ('The Real Thing')

Dear Mum

I'm not really sure how to start this.

Part of me is overthinking about how to best censor it, because it's being published and anyone can read it, and I want to ensure you don't feel uncomfortable about anything I might write ... Because I love you so much. And I'm sorry.

I'm sorry that your heart got broken all those years ago.

I'm sorry that we can't go back in time.

I'm sorry it all hurt so very much.

But I really am okay. I think I turned out pretty well, and our relationship is pretty fucking wonderful to be honest (sorry for swearing).

I just really want you to take more credit for helping me become who I am. You created me, you are such a big part of me, and all the greatness that I have experienced in my life is because I'm your daughter. Sure, it's not all been greatness, but whose life has?

And let's not forget, we are both products of one of the most glorious women we've ever known – Nana. So that's put us both in good stead in the world.

I think it's time for all of us to let go.

But especially you.

The boys and I are all well into our 40s now (argh!), and we are doing just fine. We really are. I think you should be extraordinarily proud that you brought three such interesting and wonderful human beings into the world, and let go of any residual sadness, regret or pain you might still carry around with you from the past. Just leave it there, and celebrate the incredible woman and mum that you are. Seriously.

You are the first person I call for advice, support or just to vent to. And you're always right. Ugh.

It's annoying because sometimes I don't want you to be, but you are.

And honestly, I mean, who takes up running in their mid-60s, then completes several marathons and wins GOLD at the World Masters Games within a few years, and is still running at least ten kilometres a day in their 70s?!?

See what I did there? I totally bragged about you publicly. I do that a lot. I tell everyone how proud of you I am, and how special our relationship is.

I should probably tell you as well.

So that's what this letter is.

A public way to show you my deep respect and love.

I hope you feel that love every day. It's strong, it's special, and it cannot be broken no matter what.

Michala xxxx

PS Tell Bill I love him dearly too. Especially for how he has loved you and stuck by you. And us. Together, you have both given us all so much.

PPS I didn't edit this letter. Much. It's a bit messy, and certainly not perfect. But so is life. And that's the beauty of it, isn't it?

Michala Banas: Helpmann Award-winning stage, film and television actor (McLeod's Daughters, Upper Middle Bogan)

Dear Mum

Mu-u-um? Dad, where's Mum? Mum, can I open your chocolate? Mum, where's my netball skirt? Mum, will you fix the hole in these pants? Mum, can you get rid of this spider? Mum, can I have a poodle for my birthday? Yeah, I *know* I promised to take care of him but, well, did I *ask* to be born?

Mum, can you stop calling to find out where I am? Do you think I don't know how late it is? You think I don't own a watch? Are you suggesting it's *my* fault I dented your car last night when that pole jumped out in front of me?

Oh, you've got a bad feeling about this guy? Oh, you weren't born yesterday? Why can't you see he's *the one*? Mum, can you come pick me up? You say I haven't cried like that since I was a baby? Well, how was *I* supposed to know he'd turn out to be a total dick? Did you know that psychologically speaking, all my decisions as an adult are your fault?

You hope I don't send you to a horrible nursing home? Surely they don't bathe *everyone* in kerosene? You're convinced I won't understand the heartache of being a mother until I am one myself? I mean, can you just chillax? What do you want me to say? Oh, right, I forgot. Happy birthday! I made you this fugly bowl.

Love

Julie

Julie Koh: award-winning author and daughter

Dear Mum

First off, you should have a statue erected in your honour for what you have had to put up with because of me and the fact that you did not disown me. You could write a book about all I put you through as a kid, being the little shit I was/still am.

Let's just say I definitely deserved the wooden spoon all those times, ha ha.

But seriously, I am so very glad and blessed to have you as my mum. You are the most beautiful and selfless person I have met.

The life lessons I have learnt from you have been extremely valuable and I would not be the person I am without you.

To become an elite athlete you have to have a great work ethic and I would have to give all thanks to you for instilling that in me; it's what enabled me to be an elite boxer.

As much as Dad tries to take the credit for my fighting and boxing ability, we both know that it came from your side, ha ha.

You have always been my best friend, even as a kid – all the times we would go fishing together, even when I would drag you outside to play some sort of sport with me. All the times I needed to be taken to sport matches or boxing training where you would drive 40 minutes each way and just sit and wait for the hour or so I would train, then drive me home, you were always there for me.

You have always been the best mum to me; even now when I'm down or need help you are the first person I call.

I will never be able to put into words how much I am grateful for all you have done and continue to do for me, and how much I love you.

So Mum, thanks for everything you have done for me, but most importantly, thanks for being my mum.

I love you, your son

Jason

Jason Whateley: Commonwealth Games heavy-weight silver medallist, Olympian, four-time amateur Australian champion and current Australian cruiser weight champion

Dear Mum

Thanks for being such a wonderful mum, for taking Rick and me by steam train to our holiday house at Victor Harbor when we were young kids, the bus trips into Adelaide, the train to the Adelaide beaches, always public transport as you never drove. They are great memories.

Thanks for sitting with me in my teens listening and taking in every word to Bob Dylan songs, sharing my passion for that music.

And thanks for your unwavering support for our decision to form The Angels and go on the road forever more. I still remember playing to a huge audience at the Arkaba Hotel in Adelaide, looking out and seeing you dancing on a table surrounded by sweaty, inebriated fans.

There are so many other things I could bring up, but overall I say thanks for being you. I'll never forget you.

John

John Brewster: one half of the Brewster Brothers, ARIA Hall of Fame inductee, renowned founding member of The Angels

Dear Mum

I love you dearly. Your constant support is amazing!

But could you please stop introducing me to random people (like your local chemist) as, 'This is my son Rick. He plays in The Angels!'

Love

Rick

Rick Brewster: one half of the Brewster Brothers, ARIA Hall of Fame inductee, renowned founding member of The Angels

Dear Mum

I love you. You know I love you. Your hugs, your laugh, your spirit of adventure, the way you approach complete strangers sometimes and talk to them as if you've been mates for years. That sparkle you get in your eyes when you're presented with a challenge, like defending our house from bushfires or hiking up steep, storm-ravaged hills in Samoa. I love how terrible you are in the kitchen, and that whenever you overboil, undercook, burn, spill and/or break things (let's be honest, a fairly regular occurrence), you just shrug your shoulders and carry on. I love that when you had that weird heart-attack-type-thing in the pool four years ago, you were more insulted than anything, because the doctors and nurses clearly hadn't heard about the two gold medals you won at the World Masters Games, and kept insisting you nearly drowned. I love how competitive you can get, be it playing golf or comparing hayfever symptoms. I love how you're always there for me, Nic and Tim – stepping up with advice, compassion and pride. I love you for showing us the world.

You're an inspiration to us all, Robbie. The way you cared for Dad. The way you carried on after he was gone. 'I have the gift of life,' I remember you saying once, 'and I'm not going to waste it.' I love that this was never even a possibility, simply because you're you. I know he'd be so very proud of everything you've achieved since you had to say goodbye.

All of that said, we really need to talk about something. A problem that's been bugging me for years. It may hit a little too close to home and change our relationship forever, but I can't hold it in any longer: it's time to let *Midsomer Murders* go.

Honestly, how many times can you watch the same episode and still be enthralled when you find out the old priest or mildly disgruntled gardener dunnit again? It's cute, the way you get excited and tell the same joke about it being the deadliest postcode in the UK and all, but honestly, enough is enough. We've been here before. Your obsession with *The Bill* still haunts me to this day, but you got over that. We got through it. I know you can do it again.

There are so many other shows out there waiting for you to adore them. Please give them a chance.

I believe in you.

Love

Jem

Jeremy Lachlan: author, anti-UK crime show advocate

Dear Mum

My first comfort. My first friend. My first love.

The way I love you used to frighten me when I was little. It was so overwhelmingly powerful and I never wanted to imagine life without you.

A woman born in the 1940s (the final year of the 1940s I can hear you iterating), you set an example as a feminist, without even being aware that you were one. You had your own career that you loved, you and Dad shared the housework, you stood up for yourself in the face of injustice – and in turn you paved the way for me to do the same. You taught me about loyalty to the ones you love. And that female friendships are so important, and need to be nurtured always. You showed me what it is to be selfless and family focused.

You were my team manager at basketball, sewed the sequins on my dancing costumes, never missed a school performance.

But most importantly you made me laugh. You let me make you laugh. You danced down the supermarket aisle. You taught me not to take myself or life too seriously.

Now it's my turn to become a mum. And I am so lucky to have you here to share this journey with. I can only hope my Baby Boy loves me half as much as I love you.

Forever your baby

Christie

Christie Whelan Browne: multi-award-winning stage and screen performer

Dear Mum

What a ride this thing called life is – you started it.

You said that as a young soul I came into the world laughing, I was in no hurry to walk because I was too busy laughing to pick myself up and explore the world, but once I did you encouraged me to go as far as I wanted.

I had wanted to be a clown and an artist but you gently persuaded me to go to university.

You told me I was given the gift of the gab – but I had the power to use it for good or evil. It was my choice. Perhaps in those high school years I used it for evil more than good.

I'm pretty sure you were surprised when I even finished school. Let alone was accepted into Melbourne Uni, and even more surprised the day that I stood there in a gown to accept my degree. And a few years ago, giving the 'occasional address' to graduating students.

Oh, you have guided me in many ways, for who you were as a business professional working with computers. You were my normal, a career woman, with a family.

You helped me discover my purpose. It took observing how I 'felt'. It took learning the hard lessons, listening for 'gold', relentless curiosity – and always asking 'why?'.

Ultimately my sense of accomplishment and contribution has come from knowing that I have the power to create my own future. You always encouraged me.

I've had many setbacks, naysayers and critics – and sometimes things just don't go to plan. I picked myself up, dusted myself off and reminded myself of my motto – 'If it is meant to be, it is up to me.' But you were always there for a 'cuddle in the kitchen'. My number one fan.

You said if I had an idea, I would need to do the hard work, back myself and never give up listening to those around me.

You inspired me to look forward, not back – there is no perfect path, there is just my path. It is the way it was meant to be.

When I faced many sliding-door moments you said to remember: there are those in life who watch what happens, those who ask, 'What happened?' and there are those who make things happen ... Be the person who makes things happen.

Thanks Mum.

Much love
The youngest

N

Naomi Simson: Shark Tank *panellist, RedBalloon founder, Big Red Group co-founder, entrepreneur, business leader, keynote speaker, author, governor of the Cerebral Palsy Alliance*

Dear Mum

I've been told to look for a woman
With a womb and Fallopian tubes,
But Jesus. Look at all these people.
How the hell does one even choose?

Oh! There's one … I think.
Nope. That's a man with long hair.
What about her? I like the look of that lady … and man.
I guess they come as a pair?

And what about that little girl?
She looks happy and safe.
Yes, I think I'd like a big sister
And a mum with a pretty face.

I'll run a quick fun check
Because I want a mum who's silly
I've been told that lots of humans these days
Are a bit … well … take themselves too seriously.

Pretty ... check. Silly ... check.

What else could she be?

What about smart, courageous, kind and strong?

Yeah. They're all things I'd like her to teach me.

Okay. I'm ready to leave this cloud now.

And there's a baby she's ready to bake.

I close my eyes and count to ten ...

Best choice I'll ever make.

Tildy x

Matilda Brown: writer, director, actor and businesswoman

Dear Mum

Well I know it's been a sore point that I've never really written a song directly about you, and Dad's had heaps, but the truth of the matter is, I've sincerely tried and failed dismally every time.

How do you attempt to write a line, a phrase or a melody that can even come close to what you want to convey? I don't know if it's my personal failing or the Aussie male's fear of intimacy with anything to do with their mums, but for me the Holy Grail of songwriting is to somehow capture what you mean to me in a song.

I don't know why it remains so elusive, gut twisting and super uncomfortable? I can only compare it to staring at the sun. You just can't do it – but occasionally you catch fleeting glimpses of the overwhelming power and the radiating light and energy of that giant orb, which (without wanting to be clichéd) is matched only (and maybe even surpassed) by a mother's love. You can feel its ancient sacredness, as common as sand, yet as divine as the bond between Mary and Jesus. The overwhelming power that made you, carried you and through pain birthed you, nurtured you, fed you, protected you, disciplined you and educated you on selflessness, sacrifice, sympathy, loyalty, respect, forgiveness and empathy, and then to do it all again and again for my siblings, your siblings, your parents, my children, close friends, strangers, Dad and now even sick koalas!?

As a school teacher in a boys' high school I often see the transition of young men entering the school totally dependent and openly in love with their mums – then as they grow, mature and become more sexually aware, you heartbreakingly see them 'shut up shop!'. They can never put their mother in the same category as other females, so for self-preservation they sever the ties, place them in an emotional air-tight box somewhere far, far away, and answer any caring, inquiring question with an impatient grunt. It's horrible to witness and it hits me with pangs of guilt and shame to know that I did the very same thing! I'm not sure the ties ever repair completely – or if they're supposed to – and you know the fault doesn't lie with the ever-forgiving mother.

So how does one even attempt to repair, rebuild, condense and encapsulate allllll of that?

Perhaps it's just primal fear that even by attempting such a Brobdingnagian task, I'd simply disintegrate.

So – for now – the cop-out is to simply offer my sincere thanks for everything that you've done and continue to do for all of us – and to say I love you very, very much!

Your son

Luke

PS And thanks for your fiery temper, small bladder, love of laughter and good music – and yes, I promise to keep working at that song!

Luke O'Shea: thirteen-time Golden Guitar-winning singer–songwriter, passionate surfer

Dear Mum

As I drove home from visiting you yesterday, I was overwhelmed with sadness. At least I was able to reassure you about the findings of your head scan. Fortunately, there was no sign of bleeding on your brain following that nasty fall a month ago. I do worry about you though. Each time you tumble, you hurt yourself. But this latest fall seems to have really knocked the stuffing out of you. You were so flat and scared, and appeared very fragile last night. Fortunately, you have four devoted sons and lots of loving friends who are in regular contact – these special bonds are vital to bolster your usual positive nature during these tricky times. And, of course, I'll check up on you regularly to make sure you get out into your beautiful garden each day, breathe in the warm scented air and soak up the glorious spring sunshine. Read a good book or put on one of your classical music CDs – Rachmaninov's Piano Concerto No. 2 always gives you a lift. And I've just realised that the latest season of *The Crown* has commenced on Netflix, your favourite. This one will keep you smiling for hours! Hopefully you have enough food and supplies to get you through the week? Please let me know if you need anything. I'm sure I can duck out to Woolies for any essentials. I look forward to our next catch-up in your kitchen, enjoying a cuppa and your famous muesli slice, still going strong 50 years later! Mena and the boys all send their love.

Stay safe and keep happy.

And no more falls …

All my love

James xo

James Muecke AM: 2020 Australian of the Year, eye surgeon and blindness-prevention pioneer

Dear Mum

After sixteen years it feels weird to be writing to you and deciding what to write about, so I guess I should tell you what is happening now in my world. Firstly, Annette and I are still happily married, which I don't imagine you expected would be the outcome. When I look back, I imagine it was difficult to accept a 21-year-old taking on the responsibility of a partner and two children but it felt right then and does to this day. It's always bothered me that the relationship between you and us didn't grow. We've been together 44 years and married for 36, with my stepdaughters Lisa and Sally Anne having a son each. William and Matthew have brought us great joy every day.

These days my career continues and it's now 50 years since I started. I've loved the diversity of performing, television newsreading and of course radio. These days I'm presenting *3AW Nights*, having been at the station since 1999 with over a decade doing afternoons where I took over from my good mate Ernie Sigley. A chance meeting with the boss of Sony

Music, Denis Handlin, sees me back in the recording studio with Mr Handlin showing great faith in a 65-year-old crooner boy. The first album will be all the music I used to sing with the guitar as a teenager ... very special!

Finally Mum, your scholastically underachieving youngest son was presented with an Order of Australia Medal. Who would have thought!

Love

Denis

Denis Walter OAM: entertainer, recording artist, TV personality,
3AW Nights host, Carols by Candlelight stalwart

Dear Mum

Hope you're well. Sorry. What a stupid thing to say. Force of habit I guess. It's been four years since she died Colin. Oh bugger it. How are you Mum? Are you okay up there in heaven? I'm assuming you made it up there. Not sure if I believe in heaven, but I think you did. And you were always a pretty decent and kind woman. You went to church for most of your life – but I think that was more for the friends and music rather than the sermons. This might be selective memory, but I always remembered you saying that you'd do what you wanted in life, then just repent on your deathbed. I guess he or she or whoever God is would have been listening to your inner thoughts anyway, and would have known that that was what you were planning. Is he or she or it reading this letter as I'm writing it, or pondering what I'm about to think and/or write? Is he or she or it listening to this sentence? That's what they told me in Sunday school. It's amazing what you remember.

Sooo. What are you up to? Do they have choirs and films and book clubs up there? Have you got a nice apartment?

What's the food like? One of my favourite Albert Brooks films is *Defending Your Life* where he dies and has to explain and defend how he lived his life – then perhaps he can move on to heaven – it's hilarious. Anyhoo, while he's there, there are restaurants he can go to, and all the food tastes absolutely amazing and you can eat as much as you want. I wish I told you to see that film. Although I also remember when I recommended *The Player* by director Robert Altman, you said it was 'stupid and made no sense'. I was a little offended by that. I wanted you to like it. I don't know why. Why do we need that weird approval from our family? Huh? Mum? I wish we'd talked about that before you died. I wish we talked about a lot of things. That's a shame. You were always such a great conversationalist. Interested and interesting. All my friends always said you were a terrific lady and they loved talking to you. I'm so proud of that. Hope you get this letter. It'll probably get there quicker than the letter I sent four weeks ago to my friend two suburbs away.

Love you Mum xx

Colin Lane: Perrier Award-winning comedian and cabaret artist, the Lano from Lano & Woodley

Dear Mum

It's been such a weird time, especially at a time when we need to be seeing you most of all. I really miss our catch-ups. It's funny, because whenever I miss Dad, Raquel will say, 'Why don't we go see your mum', and that always makes me feel happy again.

We talk about you all the time, we learn so much from you, and Raq loves hearing all the stories about you and Dad, and all of us boys when we were growing up.

I think you have been an amazing influence on Raq, I know she is always listening to the things you tell her about you and Dad ... she is so much like you.

I only wish Raquel had met Dad, but she says she feels like she knows him anyway, and that she can see so much of how you describe Dad to her ... in me ... in you ... and in all of us boys.

I know you worry about us boys, and how we will all be one day. I want you to know we will always be close, and look out for each other.

I just think to myself, Dad must be patiently waiting for you … like he always has ☺.

You and Dad are such an inspiration to Raq and me. Sometimes it's as though when I look at Raquel … I am Dad, looking at you. I think of Dad every day, mainly when I look in the mirror. I love it when you say how much I look like Dad, and how my voice is so similar, albeit without his soft English accent.

A little while ago, I was reading Dad's book again, when I realised something very special. Not sure if you remember the part in his book where Dad tells the story of his grandmother taking him to London to buy his first trumpet, and that the salesman was some famous jazz muso, and he gave Dad advice about the trumpet's mouthpiece being so important, so Dad ended up buying this top-of-the-range mouthpiece. Dad told me he kept that his whole life, and used it with every trumpet he ever had.

It was only after reading his book again that I realised it was that same mouthpiece Dad gave me a few years before he passed away. It sits on my dresser, and I keep some of my rings on it – one that was Nanna's wedding ring, and another that I've had since I was a kid too. It's all nice energy.

Another thing I recently found was one of Dad's cufflinks. I only have one of the pair, but I love it so much. Do you remember those gold cufflinks he had with the head of a man, wearing a turban made out of a tiny shell? They were really ornate, and I think I remember Dad telling me they were awarded to him in the '50s for 'excelling' at his job back then. I wonder whatever happened to that trophy he had too, 'Man of the Month' I think it said; it was so grand looking with a fancy marble base, and a gold figure of a man in a suit holding a briefcase, wearing a 'Bogart' hat.

I really cherish the memories, and Raq also keeps every little thing you've given her over the years too ... I know why.

Well, looks like things are settling down a bit with work etc., so we can resume our catch ups and talk about all the things we always do. I know it's mainly you and Raquel that do the talking, but it makes me so happy hearing the stories ... and advice. Raq is taking it all in ... and I know why.

Anyway Mumma, love you ... and we'll see you soon.

Briany x

PS You know that time the shed accidentally caught on fire, incinerating my mini bike, and almost the house? Well, that was the result of me playing with matches ... not sure I ever fessed up.

Brian Canham: lead singer, guitarist, composer, producer and founding member of Pseudo Echo

Dear Mum

Well, that's what I'd like to call you, where I'd prefer us to be, but I know you won't be having it. I can feel the flinch from here! The entire win of adopting out your baby is *not* being a mother, eh, so fair play. It's the game plan you make, when you're a shy girl just out of your seventeenth year, abortion's not yet legal, and you find yourself thoroughly knocked up after a date or two with the town pants man. I'm sure he was charming and persuasive, because fuck bois always are, but in 1960s regional England there were consequences, none of them great.

I admire your determination to wrench your life back. You saw single-motherhood beckoning and gave it a hard pass. You were bold and a bit nuts, heading off alone to a hastily sourced summer job in another region, no plan beyond 'Mum mustn't know, she will make me keep it.' An opportunity arose, you neatly offloaded me to a barren older couple, and home you trotted, mission accomplished, no one the wiser. Power move, girlfriend! Kudos! I would have done the same!

Well, adult me would. Looking back on seventeen-year-old me, not so much. I was too inhibited to even get laid, let alone propel myself on a reckless escapade that, frankly, would make a killer coming-of-age indie film. You just … lied and left. Went it alone. Worked hospo for months at a Butlin's holiday camp, refusing to acknowledge your burgeoning despair and waistline. Total respect. But you were the youngest of nine, and there's a freedom in that. I wound up an only child, and my conservative parents would have just as soon eaten our golden retriever, Prince, as let me waltz off like that.

I mirrored you when I eventually returned to the UK, solo, on the quest to find you, my 'real' mother. Took me nine gestational months to locate you, make contact, get to know you, and it was *lovely*, actually, for quite the while – years – until it wasn't. When you withdrew the second time I learnt the most about you. Your ambivalence about being found had a long tail, and you threw me so far from you the first time, I don't think the momentum allowed you to bring me back in.

I'm your only daughter, and your eldest, and it must cost you to pretend I'm not here. But it's also an old, familiar pain, shaped to your skin, easier than the fresh wounds and hard work of a new relationship. 'I can't give you what you want,' you said, via a relayed email, which is pithy to be sure but ingenuous. I had no idea what I wanted, was happy poodling along, and I think you were afraid to find out. Mistakes were made. And for the ones I made, I'm sorry.

You're not my 'real' mum, of course, as you didn't raise me, but the paradox is that it's not an opt in or out. You just *are*. Biology is a thing. I wish we'd been able to work towards whatever we could have been. Friends? Weird intimate strangers? The kind of plant that grows when it's planted in the wrong soil and watered intermittently but still flowers because it is hardy? Ah well. What I wanted, I realise, is to *belong*, and that's off the table. So my job is to be okay with this being how things are. Keep calm and carry on. Lucky I come from good English stock.

This isn't goodbye though. Soz. You've closed the door, yes, but self-evidently, I'm still here. I always will be, because biology. Maybe it's not you that I miss, but my idea of you, just as it's not me you've rejected, but your idea of me. And it is okay that this is how things are.

Take care, Bessie.

Love

Fiona

Fiona Scott-Norman: cabaret director, performance maker, DJ, MC, columnist, broadcaster, published author with a demonstrated interest in chickens

Dear Mum

Thank you for the laughs. Now let me be clear so Dad doesn't think I am playing favourites, I am not saying you are the 'funny parent' over the other, but what I am saying is simply, thank you for the laughs. Specifically, your laugh.

Nothing makes me smile more than your laugh. It's as infectious as 2020. Your laugh makes me smile until my smile becomes a chuckle until the chuckle becomes a cackle and we are both gasping for heavenly air.

Sometimes you laugh at my jokes, my brother's or sister's jokes, sometimes you laugh hardest at your own jokes. Often your jokes are a little saucy as Dad cries 'inappropriate for the dinner table darl', which in my mind always makes them funnier. Your whole body joins in. Your shoulders bob up and down like buoys on Sydney Harbour, your hands move to cover your reddening face. You rock back and forward.

And then there is the snorting. Your glorious snort which makes you laugh even more as the room erupts and eagerly awaits the second snort like kids waiting for the next bang of fireworks on New Year's Eve.

I don't think I know anyone who has laughed so many happy tears. Of course, there have been sad tears along the way. Parents, sisters, friends lost, but you have always found your way back to those happy tears.

I remember the first time I saw you laugh with zero abandon. You were watching John Candy with Chevy Chase on the rollercoaster at Walley World. You rode and snorted every up and down of that bumpy fun-park ride. And then there was your favourite, Fraaaank. Martin Short's barely legible wedding planner in *Father of the Bride*. How you snorted. How you cried. Every single time. Your own impression of Fraaaank would set you off again and in turn everybody else.

Mum, your laugh didn't just bring joy and comfort to our house. It was what made me fall in love with laughter. Laughter I now spend my days, my life chasing.

Thank you … LOL.

Pete

Peter Helliar: aka 'Strauchanie', comedian, children's book author, TV regular (The Project, Rove)

Dear Mum

I've been staring at this blank piece of paper for a while, because words will not truly articulate the meaning you have in my heart.

So grounded and level-headed, how did I get so lucky to have you as my greatest role model? The mother of three boys at times challenging. Maybe scrap the 'at times', who am I kidding? Dad and you together have shown us how to be men.

Every day I'd see you get up and train, prepare three boys for school, get yourself ready for work, drive us to and from sport, prepare dinner, clean the house and help us boys wash up.

Never once in my life have I been scared to tell you something, never once have I felt judged. You have helped me accept myself and everything I am. You have always been there when times have been tough. You inspire me to be more and always search for better within myself. Thank you for always being my rock and thank you for helping create a mindset that I could be anything I want to be.

Here's to plenty more years of loving animals, lolly pastilles, dim sims, chats in the kitchen and chasing passions.

Love your best-looking son

Harry

Harry Garside: Australian boxer, Commonwealth Games gold medallist

Dear Mum

I went past our old place in East Kew last week. I had taken the kids to the park nearby and as we drove down Kayhill Drive, I was pointing out all the neighbours' houses which looked so much smaller than I had remembered.

Shirley's place has had a facelift. She always did say she wanted a verandah and it looks like she finally got one. Except Shirley's speech impediment always meant she pronounced her v's and th's as b's, so her 'berandah' looks pretty good.

Branco's place is still an empty shell; doesn't look like anyone's lived in it for years, but Hazel and Jim are still there. I didn't knock on the door this time because you and I both know Hazel loves a chinwag. (Didn't we used to call her 'Have-A-Chat' for a time?)

Interestingly the old 'drug house' on the corner has been completely demolished. I was surprised to see that, since it was the kind of house that was perennially being rented out because it was so cheap. Its dilapidated roof tiles, overgrown garden and broken fences brought the entire street down.

We called it the 'drug house' because the calibre of tenants it attracted all looked like they were a 'bit rough', and there seemed to be an ongoing succession of them.

Whenever we drove past the house, you would always mutter a few choice words under your breath about the 'undesirables'.

It wasn't until the early '90s when those long-haired louts (*your words*) moved in that you really got your back up.

You, Shirley, Hazel and Branco would all stand around your front yards gossiping about the new rude blokes who spoke in four-letter words, parked their V8 hotted-up Monaros and Geminis across the nature strips and blocked old Mrs Gregory's driveway.

When I cut my foot on broken glass from one of their many smashed-up Southern Comfort bottles which lined the footpath, you'd had enough. You sent Shirley's husband, Hans, over to 'have a talk' with the four foul-mouthed men about their littering, all-day partying and the ever-growing number of cars, clogging up our beloved Kayhill Drive.

I personally would have been shaking if Hans had paid me a visit. He was a tall, stocky Bavarian man, and not one to suffer fools. Shirley, with the way she spoke, would always refer to him as her 'Big Barbarian'. I'm not sure if Hans's stern words and thinly veiled threats made much difference to the renters from hell, but for a while there, the loud music (always metal), the strewn fag buts and bottles on the street seemed to have stopped.

It was Branco, our Croatian neighbour next door, who first mentioned something was going on with the cars around the drug house. He'd seen a growing number of luxury vehicles parked in the street, and he loved his cars. Branco came over one night and told you he was sure there was something dodgy going on. He couldn't work out what was being done to the cars but they'd be parked in the street for a few days and then disappear. It was all very odd.

Mum, I have to say, you were on to it. I have this recollection of you creeping down Kayhill Drive around nine one summer evening still wearing your apron and house scuffs. There was a pen and paper in one hand and an Eveready nine-volt battery torch in the other. You left the front door open so Claire and I followed behind at a distance, curious as to what you were up to.

'Get back inside!' you hissed.

'Mum, what are you doing?' I whispered.

'Nothing. Get back inside now!'

Claire and I scampered back, just enough to watch you from the front porch. Like a housewife detective, you started writing down all the makes and models of the expensive cars haphazardly parked, which you knew didn't belong to anyone else in the street.

On the kitchen bench next to the phone, you kept the investigative notepad and every evening after dinner, you'd be out there writing everything down and then reporting back to Branco and Shirley, on hour-long phone conversations afterwards.

'Beberley, hab you called the Kew police yet?' Shirley asked one day.

'They're coming tomorrow.'

My memory of what happened next is a little hazy but the article from the newspaper was proudly cut out and stuck to our fridge for a time: 'Kew local busts statewide prestige car ring'.

It turned out these long-haired louts were actually clever dicks. They were stealing luxury cars, taking them back to the drug house at Kayhill Drive and removing both the VIN number and the rego plates. The cars would then be given new number plates and sold on to crime gangs. Your meticulous book keeping and snooping skills meant the cops had records of the make, model, previous registration and new rego. It was pretty impressive stuff.

There was a blaze of flashing lights and sirens the day those guys got busted. Branco was filming it on his Betacam.

The incident wasn't really spoken of again, although Hans did say to me afterwards, in his thick accent, 'Your mum. Very intelligent lady.'

I tried to find the newspaper article recently, but it was such a long time ago. I've told my kids about the 'drug house' and they sometimes ask about the time Gran put some 'robbers in jail'.

So, as I was saying, they've completely demolished the drug house. There's a McMansion on the corner now. It's a great big, red brick monstrosity with tall black gates and a double garage. Old Mrs Gregory's house has also been remodelled, although she left the street years ago; probably before Branco moved to Templestowe.

But Shirley is still there. She waved to me from her new 'berandah'. Sadly, her 'Big Barbarian', Hans, passed some years back, but Shirley still keeps up on the gossip of Kayhill Drive, along with Hazel and Jim.

She asked after you, Mum. I stalled the car just enough to say that you are well and that you send your love.

'Gib her my lub too, Jane. It's neber been va same here since you all moobed away.'

She's a classic, that Shirley.

Love

Jane xx

(NB – The street name has been changed to protect my former neighbours.)

Jane Gazzo: 3RRR, Triple M and BBC broadcaster, author, MC, guest speaker and co-host of 90's cult TV show Recovery

Dear Mum

I'll never forget your tears on Christmas Day.

You used to love the show-and-tell part of the day – when we'd hold up the presents we'd received and pretend that we really liked what Cousin Donna had given us.

But this day, the tears were streaming down your face. 'Come on,' I joked, trying to lighten the mood, 'surely our presents weren't that bad!'

I thought of you, Mum, when I went to Kmart to do some Christmas shopping. I walked down a street I'd never visited before and I noticed a small weatherboard house with a bench seat on the verandah. On the seat sat a big blue teddy bear. He had a Richmond beanie on his head and a handwritten name tag on his chest. His name was Timmy.

It made me smile. This was something that you'd do, Mum. Not the Richmond beanie – you never really cared for footy – but naming a teddy bear and sitting him proudly in the garden where he would keep you company ... that was something you would do.

I returned on Christmas Eve and left a box of chocolates in the letterbox. *Merry Christmas, Timmy.*

Whenever I ventured down that street – just a few times a year – I'd smile and think to myself: 'I'll see you at Christmas, Timmy.'

My Christmas Eve routine became dinner with my mate Pat at his Nonna and Nonno's house and then I'd sneak over to Timmy's place – usually around 2 a.m. – and quietly place a bag of presents inside the front gate.

The gifts became more 'extravagant' as each year went by. As well as chocolates, I'd include some lollies and a Christmas CD (I'm sorry for the Bob Dylan Christmas album, Timmy; I'm not sure what I – or Bob – was thinking).

I'd also include a card and say something like, 'Dear Timmy, I hope you've been good this year, though I see that you're still barracking for Richmond. Merry Christmas and Go Bombers!'

I never knew who lived with Timmy, and all they knew about me was I was an Essendon supporter with questionable music taste, but after Christmas they would post a note on the front door: 'Timmy says thank you.'

A couple of years ago, I ventured to Timmy's place after a particularly big Christmas Eve celebration. Nonno is a fan of a potent Italian liqueur named Centerba. 'It means 100 herbs,' he'd inform me as he refilled my glass. 'It's good for you.'

In my drunken state that night, I was carrying my bag of presents – a Haigh's Christmas stocking, a panettone, a little Bombers bear and a Neil Diamond Christmas album. But I couldn't find Timmy's house. Did I have the right street? I looked around, slightly disoriented. Yeah, this was the right street and the right house. But the seat had gone and the house had been painted.

Timmy had moved.

I carried the presents home and sat on the couch in the dark. I was mourning my mate Timmy. But really, I was missing you, Mum. It's strange what we do to maintain a connection. For me, it was a teddy bear named Timmy and his owner, who I never saw but who I imagined was a woman like you.

With Timmy gone, my mind returned to that Christmas Day more than two decades before. You looked well, Mum, but you knew that the cancer had returned. You were crying because you knew that this would be your last Christmas.

Thanks Timmy, for helping me deal with my grief. Sure, we had our differences when it came to the footy, but we were mates.

You would have liked him, Mum.

Jeffrey

Jeff Jenkins: music journalist, bestselling author, ghost writer, editor, script consultant, radio presenter, panellist, Australian music columnist

Dear Mum

You probably didn't realise how much you encouraged me to take the direction I did in life. You sowed the seed. Or maybe you knew, but we never talked about it. Anyway, throughout my life, I have often said that you always saw the bright side of things. For example, in a drought you would see an upside-down moon and say it was a sign of rain. 'See, the water will pour out.' Also, you always saw the good side of people; never being critical except when speaking of your father-in-law.

While Dad taught me to play ukulele, it was you who encouraged me to go on stage as a little boy. It was you, side stage, who caught me yawning with nerves. You said, 'That's good; yawning is good for your voice.' You always matched Dad with your soprano singing. I don't know why it bothered you that Dad didn't praise your talent. You were both quite well known equally in our farming district as a beautiful duo. He had more confidence, that's all.

I sometimes had the feeling that you and Dad thought you both missed your calling as entertainers. Perhaps you did.

You were good enough, but I assure you that very few people made a career out of singing in your era. All of us five boys are thoroughly grateful that you were successful farmers. You gave us a beautiful balance of work ethic and music and, of course, a beautiful life in the bush. I don't know where my songs would have come from without it.

Clothing us in fancy-dress competitions or encouraging artistic creations meant we were never bored. You even wrote little poems with illustrations. I wear a tropical shirt sometimes and think, wow! Look at Shirley coming out in me again ... covered in flowers!

John

John Williamson AM: multi-award-winning true-blue Aussie icon, ARIA Hall of Fame inductee

Dear Mum

The following piece has only recently been discovered and was written by Sunny Leunig in his mother's womb. A short apology letter composed by Sunny three months before his birth. A time many regard as when he was at his peak and showed the most potential in life.

It's now 87 days until I enter this world and God, I'm so sorry for what is coming.

Nice try but giving me a name like *Sunny* won't stop me from being quite a sombre, dark and generally gloomy child. Unfortunately, this won't change that much as I move through adulthood. There will be no *sunny disposition* and I hope you can excuse me for this.

I would also like to pre-emptively apologise for the awful chaos and many fights between myself and older brother, Gus. I would like to prepare you for our infamous great backyard sibling cricket championships of 1989. It will be an emotionally charged series where cricket bats will be hurled, windows will be broken, punches will be thrown, and piercing screams and obscenities will echo throughout our small hometown of Euroa.

I'm sorry for the time our fighting will lead us to being hauled into line by security at the National Gallery for knocking a priceless painting off the wall. I guess I'm just sorry for you having to bear the burden of single-handedly raising two difficult and often troubled children.

I would like to also quickly apologise for all the usual stuff like the underage drinking and smoking, the endless tantrums, the troubles with the law, the constant whingeing, the poor grades, the bong water stains on the carpet and the many hours of profound stress and worry I will inflict on you in the future.

But I would also like to say thank you. Because, despite all my despicably appalling behaviour, you will somehow always love me unconditionally. You will also teach me the ways of the world, constantly holding my hand through the dark, and show me the value and wisdom of holding tolerance and respect towards others.

I will witness your own pain and heartbreak, and we will go through much sadness together. I promise that through these experiences we will build an unbreakable bond that will last forever.

Without you knowing, I will often look at you with admiration and see the woman who persevered through many difficult challenges just to provide me and my brother a decent life. When I am rich and successful, I will pay you back. Actually, that rich and successful bit won't have happened by the time you read this letter but trust me – I can see into the future.

So, despite not being born yet, I wish to say that I love you already. This love will keep growing into something even stronger than the very forces that created the cosmos.

In the meantime, on behalf of my future self – thank you and I'm sorry.

Love

Sunny x

Sunny Leunig: filmmaker and magosopher (a cross between a magician and a philosopher)

Dear Mum

You have spent your life leading by example which has resulted in a tribe – five children, eleven grandchildren and eleven great-grandchildren (to date) – who all understand what it means to care for themselves, their family and their community.

You have always put family first and your loyalty and commitment could never be questioned. You recently sent me a box of Anzac biscuits for my birthday, which took me straight back to my days living in London. The Anzac biscuit care package would arrive every couple of months, without fail, and my housemates and I would inhale them in one sitting. I swear you could sell that recipe for millions!

You are famous in our family for the wise words you have written in our birthday and Christmas cards over the years – from Shakespeare to Confucius to Socrates to Anon. We've laughed at some of them but overwhelmingly we've benefited from the wisdom.

Not only have you filled the lives of your family members with love and support, you have also been a lifelong and tireless advocate for your community. Everything from the local football and netball club to the school to a suite of charities, they have all benefited from your support, fundraising and advocacy. In turn, the community has benefited, and as we all know, strong communities provide another level of support and satisfaction to their members.

In fact, I remember at one point you were involved with so many committees, boards, charities and volunteer organisations that Dad leant over to me at the kitchen table and said, 'She's like salt and pepper your mother ... she's on everything.'

Not only has your charity work been a cornerstone of your life, you have always defended the underdog and stood up to bullies. I personally witnessed this many times over the years, with just a few examples here:

- The time you strolled into 'Speaker's Corner' at Old Parliament House in Adelaide and stood toe to toe with the leader of National Action telling him exactly why his racist ideals were wrong. The fact that men with swastika tattoos surrounded you didn't bother you. For the record, it bothered me heaps and I was terrified!
- The multiple occasions you have written letters to the editor calling out homophobic and racist opinions.
- That time you invited some Afghan refugees up to the house for a BBQ to make them feel welcome in town.

You are far from an agitator but you will never stand by and watch while the powerful, the privileged and rich take advantage, malign or marginalise those who are less fortunate.

I should finish this by pointing out that you also have a glorious sense of fun, you love telling jokes and making people laugh. And I feel sure that if you had just one wish it would simply be for everyone to be happy ... or for me to win Lotto!

Thank you for providing such a shining example ... and for the Lotto win ... if it happens!

Much love.

Your son

Anthony

Lehmo: full-time funny person, radio host, TV presenter, author, occasional actor

Dear Mum

Is it okay if I call you that?

You've been a mum to me since we first met a few weeks before I turned nineteen. You've been the only 'mum' to me since then. Someone once told me that I'd bummed out with both my parents and there was no hope for me, but I think I've done all right finding you.

A few years ago, I found out that the expression 'blood is thicker than water' is actually 'the blood of the covenant is thicker than the water of the womb'. It means the opposite of what I was always told it meant. The bonds we make are stronger than the bonds we are born with.

Your kids are lucky to have been born to parents like you and 'Dad', but for someone like me, there is something quite comforting in the original expression. We don't have to hold on to negative relationships simply because of biological bonds.

I was scrolling through Instagram yesterday when I came across a quote someone posted from my book *If I Wake*. It's one of those inspirational quotes floating around on the internet, but it fitted my story, my main character, and how I feel about family.

'Family aren't always blood. They're the people in your life who want you in theirs; the ones that accept you for who you are. The ones who would do anything to see you smile and who love you no matter what.'

Thanks for checking up on me over the years, being there for me, offering advice when I need it, and always having an open door and a bed to crash on when I happen to be passing through your state. Thanks for being my mum.

Love

Nikki Moyes

Nikki Moyes: young-adult fiction author

Dear Mum

I miss you. I haven't seen you since the Woodford Folk Festival last Christmas. The pandemic is keeping us apart. But I keep thinking about that first morning at the Woodford campsite after our first night's sleep. I came into your tent to see how you were. I could see things weren't great. The big blow-up 'Euro mattress' I'd given you had all but deflated, leaving you mostly on the ground. You said, 'Well to tell you the truth darling, I've had quite a night of it.' You hadn't slept at all. Well before midnight you'd needed to go to the toilet but the toilet blocks were a long way away in a dark campground we didn't know our way around, so you'd been holding on. Then you got very cold because I hadn't thought to show you where the extra blankets were (the cold night had surprised us). You were 78 years old and this was the first of seven nights camping. And yet, when you were telling me these things, peering up with your cute old person's face and your grey hair all wispy, swaddled in the meagre cotton blanket with your bum on the ground and your head and feet up, jackknifed in your useless airbed, you were laughing. Laughing! Giggling with the joy of a twelve-year-old. Tears were streaming down your face and as you told me about each new night-time horror, you laughed even more. I marvelled at you that morning, but I wasn't surprised Mum. This has always been you.

Laughter and joy.

But how?

Eighteen months before I was born, Richard, your beautiful first-born boy, died of cot death. And yet the only world I've known, the world you showed me, is a world without danger, a world of hope and happiness, a world that will smile at me if I'm brave enough to smile at it. How did you do that, when every time I went to sleep, it must have been the most terrifying thing in the world for you? But as a boy, when I closed my eyes, the last thing I would see was your loving eyes, your gentle smile, no shadow of grief. And when I woke up, there you were, ready to take my little hand and throw ourselves into the wondrous surprises of every day. You're with me in every breath. You are with me when I burst with the joy of being alive. You are with me when I'm fearful for my boys but keep it to myself. And you will be with me when I'm so sad I can't see a way forward, but need to press on for others.

After that first night of no sleep at Woodford Folk Festival, you wandered around the festival all day, seeing things you'd never seen before, joining the choir so you'd be part of the closing ceremony, doing dance classes, getting a massage! We hiked up the steepest part of the hill (again, my fault, there were easier routes) to watch the opening ceremony and hear the Woodford message of a brighter future for our planet.

Then you and I walked back to the campsite holding hands and, with just a few minor adjustments to the previous night's debacle, you climbed into your camp bed and I kissed you good night like you used to kiss me. You slept ten hours straight, woke up refreshed and excited, ready to share the next week of festival life with Ado and me and the boys and our camping buddies, a 78-year-old woman, delighting and intriguing and comforting and enriching everyone lucky enough to spend time with you.

I love you Mum. Everybody does.

Rob

Rob Carlton: Logie Award-winning actor, writer, MC, director–producer

Dear Mum

'I wish the fairies would come and clean this house.'

I swore I'd never say that when I became a mother because seriously 'fairies'? ... We knew you were referring to us kids who needed to 'pull our weight'.

You love an old expression and when sitting down to write this letter, I thought of the times you've gotten us through situations both good and bad with a quote from the vault.

Our shared middle name is from an old saying, 'Sugar for Joy', but the first one *I* can remember hearing was: 'You're a cat, you only come around for hugs when *you* want them.' I'm allergic to cats so I never understood it, but as a mother faced with the devastating reality of my boys leaving me, I too have uttered that exact proverb. They didn't get it either.

Growing up, all naughty deeds that a young Amber Joy committed were met with, 'A little birdie told me ...' I never looked at birds the same way again. Their betrayal was always at the forefront of my mind, not knowing at the time, it was your cover-up for a dibber dobber.

Later, I learnt 'Blood is thicker than water' after leaving in a trail of dust with my 'one true love' that ended with a bawling phone call to you, and me being back in my childhood bed. Right again Mum with, 'Darling, leopards don't change their spots' and 'Only a mother knows.'

My favourite: 'If you marry for money, you'll earn every cent.' Duly noted and completely safe. First date memories (with my now husband) was in a mate's borrowed BMW and a debt to his sister for $2000. If I was to 'earn every cent', I pretty much had him paid off in the first few weeks. Thanks Mum.

A strong work ethic was instilled in part by your encouragement to 'Keep the wolves from the door' so that we'd never know the heartache of 'When money walks out the door, love flies out the window.' Truthfully, I never understood this, due to the fact that it was never delivered the same way: love was flying out of windows and money was walking in and out of doors and poverty wasn't even sure whether it was required in the saying anymore. For the record Mum, the old proverb is, 'When poverty comes in at the door, love flies out the window', and now I get it.

We'd all like to leave this world with a legacy and this Mum could be yours. It's your 'tried and true' gift to the family, and something special we can turn to when we're going through our own 'trouble and strife'.

I've just returned home from my country music life on the road to a very messy house and I fought the words as they left my mouth, 'I wish the fairies would come and clean this house ...'

Love

Amber Joy

Amber Joy Poulton: Top 10 Australian country music charts singer–songwriter

Dear Mum

I'm writing this having been to visit you this afternoon, though I'm not sure you remember.

That's not a reflection at all on your still razor-sharp mind, which I regularly exercise by forcing you to do the *Times* cryptic crossword, much to your feigned dismay! But you'd put your back out and despite your regular, warrior-like entreaty of 'I'm all right mate', as I was leaving, the Endone was just kicking in and, to be honest, you had started to fade towards the tail of the conversation.

It was an amazing chat. I was telling you about my plans for my next book and the bit I was going to write about teaching maths to really young kids – spatial reasoning, developing a sense of number – the usual nerd shit I go on with. And you recounted a story about me as a very young kid. Reminded me how I'd nearly died from a couple of brain seizures when I was new born, had the last rites read to me and all manner of intense stuff. I was familiar with that, albeit some of the intimate details were new.

But then you told me how you'd coached me intensely for the first couple of years in all that sort of early maths stuff. That because of genuine fears I might have suffered brain damage, you were in constant contact with a paediatrician, getting exercises for me to do, to make sure I hit all the developmental guidelines you were worried I might never make. It was an amazing story from my childhood that I don't think you'd ever shared before.

And it got me thinking about your childhood. I know it was really tough and that you showed incredible guts to get where you did. I can remember, when I was about seven or eight, overhearing you fighting with your mum once and it seemed to be about whether she'd been there for you as a mother should. You faced many other challenges that I vaguely know about, and I think you think I might vaguely know about, but of which I know none of the details. But to be really honest, I know very little about the story of your life.

Part of me really wants to know these things about you. Part of me is worried perhaps the last thing you'd want to do is go there. But as I move into a beautiful, happy new phase in my life and find out more about my new partner and the amazing life she has led, I'm thinking about this sort of stuff and wanting to share in the richness of other people's stories.

So Mum, I'll be really honest with you. There are so many things I want to ask you about your life; so many questions I have. But I've got no idea if you'd be cool with that or if you'd rather not revisit some of the bumps you've had to ride out. That's why I slid you a copy of this book. I assume you'll skip the wonderful contributions of Amanda Keller and Larry Emdur and come straight to my bit.

So the next time we catch up, for a crossword and complaining (x), if you're happy to talk about your life, just say. If not, don't mention anything and I'll just pretend that you started with that dishy Guy Pearce's letter and haven't gotten to mine yet.

I couldn't love you more Mum ... thanks for everything.

Adam S

Adam Spencer: author, comedian, radio announcer, TV personality, Redkite board member, Fred Hollows Foundation ambassador, maths geek

Dear Mum

To this day, I believe that if you had given me the wallet with the velcro that I wanted SO desperately for my tenth birthday, my childhood would have been complete. But I got the boring one with the zip, because you worried I might lose the few coins I had saved. We both know it was hard for me to get over. I love you for still trying to make it up to me by buying me wallets with velcro well into my 40s, but it's just not quite the same.

I believe your secret strategy of coming home late from your friend's house and quickly setting the table – making your hungry family believe that dinner was under control – was actually a genius move. When really, you were just trying to buy yourself some time, secretly scratching your head while you 'shook the fridge' to see what would fall out that you could quickly concoct.

I believe that growing up in an 'open house', where everyone was always welcome for a drink, dinner or even my best mate moving in to live with us for a year, was beautiful.

I'm sorry I didn't tell you she was a vegetarian for the first three months, but the dog loved the secret treats under the table.

I believe it was very kind of you to let me borrow your car the day I got my licence. I am forever grateful you did not tell Dad I scraped all four panels down a pole – and you secretly got it fixed.

I believe I could never have bought my little business at the age of eighteen without your unwavering support. I believe it was so wrong that in the early days when money was tight, I would get my little brother to syphon petrol out of your car when you were not looking (until he got a mouthful of petrol and would not do it for me anymore). Thanks for laughing about that when you found out.

I believe we have had the greatest adventures selling muesli at trade shows all around the world together. But you telling potential clients that the queen feeds it to her corgis was pushing the truth boundaries a little too far.

I believe you have always been the most incredible mother, friend and confidante to me and I am truly the luckiest daughter ever (well, if I had got that velcro wallet I would have been).

I love you Mummy dearest.

Love, your best little knitter

Carolyn xxx

Carolyn Creswell: entrepreneur, founder of Carmen's, 2012 Telstra Australian Business Woman of the Year, ambassador for the Asylum Seeker Resource Centre, proud mother of four young children

Dear Mum

I am wondering if this letter falls under the 'Facebook rule', which is 'Do not make fun of your mother on Facebook'. But what may appear as *making* fun is, I promise, just *having* fun. You are a very funny person, often unintentionally, and we are a funny family. A friend of mine would beg for the next instalment of the 'Les and Sally Show' after my visits home, whether that be a mishearing or mispronunciation or the latest accidental poisoning. And, trust me, I do all the same things: I have your slight lisp and tendency towards spoonerisms. Did I tell you that when we were in New Zealand, I asked the way to 'Parthur's Arse' instead of 'Arthur's Pass'?

Anyway, I'll resist poking fun. There's something more serious I want to say: I miss you. It's been a long time. My last trip home hardly counts, since it was such a disaster. Five days to give you both a break: Dad from being bored and sick, and you from looking after Dad. And then I got food poisoning on the plane and spent the entire stay hugging the toilet bowl upstairs while Dad convalesced downstairs. After, of course, we laughed about it.

It's a stereotype that daughters fear turning into their mothers, but in this case, I reckon it'd be pretty great. Going to talks on the history of paper and other obscure subjects, walking at *least* three kilometres a day, and assigning holiday destinations a score from one to five choc-bombs, 'just like the film reviewers in the paper'. Can't wait.

Thanks Mum, for being unapologetically you. I wouldn't have it any other way.

Charlotte

Charlotte Guest: writer and bookseller

Dear Mum

I adore you. You know that.

You're the most considerate and strong woman I've ever met. And you are so brave.

As a kid, I remember watching you play soccer. You were goalkeeper and absolutely fearless. You'd run at players, dive at the ball, fly-kick referees ... you were a mad talent. It wasn't until I was older that I realised you were on performance-enhancing drugs.

Turns out that water bottle was full of scotch and you were necking liquid courage the whole time.

Either way, I still think you're a fearless, strong woman and I look up to you. And as I reach the stage in my life where I too will join you in the ranks of mums, it makes me wonder ... what sort of mum will I be. Because when you think about it ... there are so many different 'mum characters' to choose from. And it's like playing Mortal Kombat or Street Fighter video games – all the characters have their strengths and weaknesses.

Here's the top four picks in Mortal Kombat – Mum Edition:

Helicopter Mum
- Special strength: knowing every move their child makes.
- Weakness: raising a dependent child who's actually fucking useless.
- Kill move: writing an angry letter to council for not having rubber matting at the playground.

Activewear Mum
- Special strength: having fifteen subscribers to her mummy blog.
- Weakness: having a kid who is actually kind of ugly, which is ruining their social media aesthetic.
- Kill move: getting a Lorna Jane–sponsored post on Instagram and a free pair of tights.

Don't Give a Fuck Mum
- Special strength: screaming at her free-range children from 100 metres away.
- Weakness: someone criticising her kids' behaviour.
- Kill move: skipping the parent–teacher meetings to binge-watch Netflix.

Rabbit Mum
- Special strength: being a cyclone at school drop-off because she has more than four kids.
- Weakness: sleep deprivation and remembering the kids' names.
- Kill move: convincing her husband to get a vasectomy. Finish him / KO!

That is totally silly. And I can imagine you rolling your eyes at me.

But Mum, I don't think I've ever told you that my confidence to be silly and do comedy comes from you. A lot of people give Dad credit for that … but you were always the one who told me I could be anything I wanted. You were always there saying 'yes' to every activity and silly game. And it's an easy choice … you're the mum character I want to be.

I love you endlessly

X Amy

Amy Hetherington: terminally positive comedian and MC

Dear Mum

I have so much to thank you for – knowing where to begin is overwhelming.

I recall so vividly my light-bulb moment when I became a mum for the first time myself ... 'I get it now' was one of my first thoughts. With you by my side I felt that instant unconditional love and the innate desire to protect and nurture, and I hoped I would follow in your footsteps.

Thank you Mum, for making me believe that tertiary study was not optional. You raised me to believe it was non-negotiable and for that I will always be grateful. There are so many sliding-door moments in a young adult's life, I'm glad that one was taken out of my hands. That was gift number one from you.

Thank you for putting up with me during my teen years – what a white-knuckle ride that must have been!

How you managed to 'lead me to water' – I often wonder as a parent now if I could do as well as you have. What's even more impressive Ma is you enrolled in university at the same time as me, taking in a whole new path yourself in your 40s.

You've always celebrated each of us being so different – I truly felt encouraged to be myself, warts and all.

I am often asked how I have so much inner strength to cope with much of what life has thrown my way, particularly in the past few years. My answer ... if you've met my parents, you'll know why.

Mum, you've shown me strength through adversity, something I now share with your grandchildren – you are a true woman warrior.

You went on to become the CEO of a successful regional job network company spanning three states, while making sure you were also a 100 per cent hands-on grandmother to my children, and a role model to all our family.

Taking annual leave from such a busy career to look after your grandchildren so I could have an annual holiday was just another example of selflessness that was a constant in your life.

You and Dad never divorced, you went your own way. I know it wasn't quite as simple for you Ma as it sounds on paper, but it did mean as my parents you always remained friends. I am forever grateful for the comfort that gave me as a child, and today, as an adult. It is a gift you just can't buy a child, and it was you who made that happen. I take my hat off to you Ma – it was such a selfless act, and trust me, it has not gone unnoticed.

You remained devoted to Dad, at his side right to the end as he battled cancer. I will never forget the look you both shared in that hospital room near the end of his life. No words needed to be spoken – that memory will remain with me forever. I witnessed two people who truly knew one another, a lifetime of memories and shared experiences that needed no words to express to each other how much it all meant to you both. That was a gift I will always cherish.

Despite you separating, your children are shining examples of the great love and wonderful friendship you and Dad shared all those years.

Ma, after years of hard work and playing catch-up, stand proud of your achievements. You're independent, a self-funded retiree, a wonderful grandmother and my treasured mentor – my go-to for everything. Thank you Ma – you truly are a one-in-a-million.

Love you Ma

Cass

Cassandra Thorburn: TV personality and mother of three

Dear Mum

I had two mothers. The birth one who made me, and the adoptive one who made me a life.

From the first one, I got the nature, not so much the nurture. I was lucky to meet you before you died, and found out that you loved Slim Dusty (like me) and that no one had a bad word to say about you. You must have loved my father because you went on to have five more children with him. Thank you for giving me a chance to walk on the earth and the chance to play music, meet Slim, form Midnight Oil and get to stick it up John Howard at the 2000 Sydney Olympics.

My adoptive mum was kind, funny and never had a bad word for anybody. When I was a child she read the *Women's Weekly* for styling tips, Charmian Clift's column in the *Herald* for women's business, Maggie Tabberer as well. We'd tune into *Beauty and the Beast* on ATN-7 where the women panellists always outfoxed the grumpy and outnumbered host. One day, on King Street, Sydney, while driving the Valiant, we nearly ran over one of the Beasts, a jaywalking Stuart Wagstaff.

Thanks Mum for the Space Food Sticks, as we were told on the TV the NASA astronauts ate them on the Apollo.

When you lost Dad it didn't take you long to get back on track, aged 77.

And thanks for the Vicks VapoRub and the Lucozade. You were there for us through every tedious school gala, nightmare, pushbike stack and fever, so that makes you the real mum.

Jim Moginie

Jim Moginie: founding member of Midnight Oil, record producer, film composer, ARIA Hall of Fame inductee and fully fledged solo artist

Dear Mum

It seems to be such a long time since you last closed your eyes. A long time yet my memories of you are so vivid.

I can remember being the smallest of kids, and you always being there. I seemed so happy to play in the backyard of the home you made for us out of the meagre pittance Dad was able to earn at his basic wage jobs. We never seemed to be poor, and yet compared with what kids have today, we thrived on the smallest of gifts.

Graeme and Lois always looked after their little brother so beautifully, and their care came I know from the teachings of a wonderful unselfish love you gave us all.

To say that you ruled the roost is an understatement. Of course, Dad was the Boss of the household, just as long as it was okay with you.

Your diminutive size belied your power in the family. Amazed I still am at the way you could gently persuade us all to your way of thinking.

I'm sure that your life was tough. As a young woman working in the woollen mills, guiding your family through the Great Depression and World War II, seeing your kids off to school then work, Graeme as a panelbeater, Lois as a comptometrist (computer operator) and me ... what on earth must you have thought when I announced I wanted to be a professional singer/entertainer? You and Dad both knew the hardships that could've come from another war or depression for someone treading the boards, but still you encouraged me. Sometimes I think that without those immense social obstacles of war and depression, you might have had a life on the stage yourself. What a beautiful voice you had. I still hear you swimming around in my head, we all loved your singing, as did your friends who gathered at our place on very regular occasions to enjoy a 'social evening'.

Mum, you might well have been only four feet eleven and three-quarters of an inch, but you lived the life of a beautiful giant.

When you passed, I said to you, 'I suppose I have to take off my training wheels now, Mum.' Well I'm still trying to learn how to ride. It's a long task and your memory and love drives me on. So, perhaps before I take my final breath I'll have achieved enough to have made you proud of me.

Your loving son

Norman John

Normie Rowe AM: the original King of Pop, singer, songwriter, actor, ARIA Hall of Fame inductee, Kidney Heath Australia patron, Vietnam veteran, Australian War Memorial national hero

Dear Mum

Remember in 1983 when I said I was glad to be born when I was born? How had people even lived without electricity, books, cars, Lego and *Star Wars*? And you raised your eyebrows and talked about acid rain, the Iron Curtain and nuclear war before putting on some footy franks.

Were you trying to prepare me for the end of the world? At eight years old? I wasn't ready for the prospect of planetary annihilation. I couldn't order ice cream without wanting to bury myself under blankets.

You died too long ago. We had three decades; it was an instant. I'm still spinning in an irregular orbit. I miss your whole-of-face smile. I miss the way you'd talk to cows you didn't even know. I miss your unscientific claim that the soul lies in people's eyes. I miss your hopeful, broken heart. I miss the way you were in the world, and the way I was with you.

There are too many holes in the fabric. I barely remember your voice. I don't remember you actually talking to cows. I just assumed. It seems like something you would have done. But somehow, across time or universes, you're in every gesture, every unexpected shaft of sunlight. We were so unprepared to lose you. But we're okay. I, for one, can order ice cream quite confidently now.

I wish you were here. And I wish you'd explained that acid rain wouldn't make the roof melt.

Love

Rhett

Rhett Davis: writer, bookseller, cardigan enthusiast

Dear Mum

You've had many lives Mum, and I'm thankful for being there for so many of them.

I missed your first life, growing up in India and England, and also the second, which I hear was carefree, happy and smashed to pieces when I came into the world screaming and shitting and crying.

I have been there for the rest, though.

I was there for your selfless and manic first Australian life.

I was there for the sad life, when you were suddenly alone in a strange city.

I was there for the resurrected life too, with your train pass and movie tickets and library books about colonial times.

And now I'm here for the best life, the happiest life, the life with the most beautiful grandchildren, the bluest oceans, the best meals and the biggest smiles.

Who'd change a thing?

Love ya Mum

Ben

Ben Mckelvey: journalist, podcaster, author, volleyballer

Dear Mum

It was 30 years ago this year that you shuffled off this mortal coil. Although it was a mighty relief to see you leave the constant, debilitating pain behind, it's difficult not to think about all the stuff we have since missed in each other. Not just because I was your favourite (which I clearly was!), but because when you passed I was, frankly, being a bit of a dick. Kicked out of school for being a little brat, sacked and arrested for stealing a carton of smokes from Coles, then just before you died, kicked out of drama school for being a big brat. I can't help but shake the feeling that when you died I was nothing more than a massive disappointment to you.

But I really, really hope that you've gotten to see me try to make a fist of it since then. I obviously have no clue as to what your vantage point has been these past 30 years, but it has never stopped me from always trying to share with you my successes. Which conversely means you have also seen all my failings too! Like that time I whipped a guy over the arse for a pair of shoes. Or the time I stole a wheelchair from a hospital and the police caught me and pushed me back while I bullshitted them mercilessly. The several times I've been arrested. The drug-fuelled orgies, dangerous motorcycle riding, and drinking my pancreas to destruction etc. etc. etc. etc. etc.

But I of course hope that you've seen some of the good stuff too. Not just the career stuff, but the life stuff. I think you would love my wife (you're both Virgos so who knows?) and I know for a fact that you would adore our daughter. I easily count her as the most successful venture I've undertaken in my life.

I know you taught me that I have to take the good with the bad, to learn from my mistakes … so maybe it ultimately isn't so bad that I've made more than my fair share.

Thanks for everything you taught me in the 22 years I knew you, Mum. I still miss you.

Much love

Steve

Steve Le Marquand: character actor

Dear Mum

A friend of yours once asked me: 'Where do all her thoughts go?'

We were sitting on the couch you carefully picked out only months earlier. We sipped tea, blinking at each other through a new wild grief.

Thirteen years later, my brothers and I keep discovering new–old pieces of you. Thoughts we didn't know you had. Letters to a friend, stilted diary entries, and – recently – an audio tape from your late 20s. You talk about an A you received on a psych exam, the nap you might take, how you'll see *Paper Moon* at the cinema. All those giggles, sighs, hesitations. All those breaths in and out.

And this: a raw scrawl of an entry in an exercise book, after visiting your dad in a nursing home. You're furious about his treatment there, and about the fact he went to war as a mere teenager. There's a word that's been added later – it hovers above 'the' and 'war'. An upwards arrow of an edit between them, pointing to the heavens. It's written with a different lilt, underlined, and the word is: 'fucking'.

I love the thought of you returning to that entry and adding 'fucking' to it. It was like discovering an underwater city. The capacity of you to be furious.

I have it too. 'FUCK, Mum,' I say out loud, and loudly, when I want to ring you up, when there's any news ever, after I wake from a dream of you. It's a roar, a sob, a tantrum; a hope for a magic spell to reappear you. I say it when 'You're the Voice' plays on the radio, when I'm in the gentle blast of a Perth sunset, when I wear your dressing gown. I say it when I get that all-over body ache that's like an urge or a charge or a call to action, something like, 'I'm sorry,' and 'I understand now,' and 'Why didn't you tell me?' and 'Thank you,' and 'Am I an okay person?' I say it when I see any mother and any daughter, doing absolutely any thing; when I ache at the incompleteness of meeting a person who'll never know you; when I want to show you what we've done, how we are, who we are.

So, dear Mum:
I (fucking) miss you.

Love

Brooke

Brooke Davis: internationally acclaimed author (translated into 20 languages), bestselling writer, bookseller

Dear Mum

Remember when those local louts pushed me off the ten-metre tower at the local baths? Reckon I was about eight. I never intended to leap off. I just wanted to climb up, touch the sky, and clamber back down.

As I peered over the edge, the diving pool was a tiny blue square below. You were a miniature LEGO person peering up. As I waved, one of the pimply teenagers nudged me off the edge. I tumbled through the sky finding neither voice nor air. Falling, falling, then *smack*! The water, hard as concrete, spanked my bottom.

I did a shaky dog paddle to the edge of the pool to the soundtrack of kids' cruel laughter. It stung more than the slap of the water. But you were there to scoop me up, wrap me in a towel and love, and instil in me a valuable life lesson: it's okay to cry but it's important to be resilient.

Through your life actions you've shown me how to overcome setbacks and soldier on in the face of adversity. Sure, you were short-changed a tertiary education. But rather than languish in the life of a Stepford Wife you took yourself back to university and obtained a PhD in gender studies – aged 70!

Only this week you rocked me in your arms as I wept over the unnecessary death of a dear mate, a true huckleberry friend. I could find neither voice nor air to express my grief. Falling, free-falling. But you were still there, decades on, wrapping me in your love. Telling me it's okay to cry but it's important to be strong.

Thank you Mum.

Love

Elise x

Elise Elliott: journalist, presenter, writer, rev-head

Dear Mum

So lovely to be in touch again Mummy.

Around the same time as your fight for life came to an end, our dear cousin Justin resigned his commission as a commando. Yesterday, his heroic and selfless dedication to his dear partner came to an end. Pinny suffered with motor neuron disease for over eight years, and Justin remained at her side throughout, as her confidant, friend and dedicated carer. Aunty Margret and Uncle Frank kept us informed of the battle Pinny endured and her courage and good humour remained right up till the end. The disease progressed to the stage where Pinny could not move, and Justin did everything for her, including getting her ready each week to watch the Tigers. He would prop her up in front of the TV and she would wear the crocheted Tigers beanie I made for her, which was touching for me. Pinny could not speak and communicated by blinking her eyes and a computer would translate her messages, which were cheery and humorous. Justin said that when Pinny recently received a personal video message from Tigers legend Kevin Bartlett, she was thrilled and could not believe her luck. Mike Brady also recorded a special video message and sang 'Up There Cazaly' for Pinny which she saw and smiled at during her last days when she was in and out of consciousness. The smiles and tears said it all.

Hearing people complain about the various issues regarding Covid seems so pathetic to me because I am reminded of what you and Daddy would always say – there are others worse off.

I will never forget the story of Pinny and Justin as long as I live. I am so proud to be part of their family and I am determined to remind my children about what others are going through.

It came time to sell our lovely property and you can imagine the conflict I had about that decision. Knowing you and Daddy made every mud brick – and my fingerprints are even on a few – made parting with it a challenge, but I am glad to say the property went to a lovely family and I am welcome to drop by anytime, which I occasionally do. I am settled in a lovely place close to where we lived growing up and the isolation does not worry me at all. I enjoy my own company, and I am relieved to be away from the falseness of the singing business. I know you and Daddy would like me to keep singing, and I have had a number of offers to record new songs and perform them online. But for now, I am more interested in keeping to myself and reflecting on how fortunate I am.

Casey is doing some wonderful art, and William and his partner, Alice, have bought their first house in regional Victoria, which is very exciting. Jess seems settled in America, and I just love receiving the regular video updates featuring little Daisy who is now four. We FaceTime regularly, and she is absolutely gorgeous. Of course, that is an unbiased view. Desie and Trish are very well also, and Desie is keeping me supplied with tomato seeds, because I want to continue the family tradition of growing my own vegetables. If that fails, the supermarket is just around the corner. I'll pop in on Glen and Marc today for a cuppa – you would love their garden.

So we are at the end of a sad week, but a very inspiring and optimistic one as well. Because of you and Daddy, I always had an optimistic outlook, and this has been reinforced by Pinny and Justin. I am fortunate to have had you and Daddy to always teach us, to remember where we came from. I do, and that's where I live now.

Danny sends his love and says he still remembers the first meal you ever cooked for him. (I wonder if that is good or bad?)

All my love to you and Daddy

Coll xx

Colleen Hewett: singer, twice Queen of Pop, actor, ambassador for Rotary's Violence Free Families

Dear Mum

Have I ever written you a letter before? Maybe one or two at uni? I think it has mostly always just been the Sunday night calls. Both of us always starting our seemingly semi-scripted chats with 'No news, really.' Putting the guidelines and barriers in place. Setting the emotional boundaries for what is allowed to follow. Then carefully treading the well-worn path: whether everyone is well, how the weather has been, how work is going.

No news, really.

Is it me or you who doesn't want to mess with that safe equilibrium? I used to think it was you. But these days I think it's me.

Something ethereal yet insurmountable feels like it's in the way for me. To move past it would maybe shatter the roles we understand, built on years of this formula – simultaneously fragile and rock solid.

I'd like to talk more deeply, but I think I need this part of my life to be stable and uncomplicated and free of surprise. Me the son, you the mum. I feel like an unseen and instantly draining energy holds me back whenever I even contemplate moving past the status quo.

A lot has happened for me behind the veil of no news, though. News has happened.

Three kids, a separation, my ongoing recovery from alcoholism, career changes, relationships, therapy, self-doubt. You know about it all; but really you don't.

Maybe more things than I realise have happened for you, too.

I'd like to know more about your depression and anxiety when I was small. The hospital stays and daily rehab. Or maybe I wouldn't. I could share the uncertainty I felt as a kid – but what's the point of that now. You don't need to know, even though you probably already do.

And you know, sometimes I feel like I just want to be eleven again. It was hard being a kid at times, but I still loved it. Less awareness, before the bondage of self. Never blissfully ignorant, though. I think I could always sense something lurking, just out of reach.

I used to like being allowed to stay up late on a Saturday night with you and Dad, to watch *The Two Ronnies*, with Chinese takeaway. Perhaps even until *Match of the Day* was on at 10 p.m., if Liverpool were playing.

Do other people wish they could go back in time? Just for a while.

It's Sunday morning here in Australia. Which means it's Saturday night where you are – maybe you and Dad are having Chinese takeaway. Watch *Match of the Day* for me.

I'll call you later tonight. No news, though.

Rob x

Rob Pegley: strategist, writer, editor, manager in media (News Limited, Bauer/ACP, SBS and more)

Dear Mum

Or 'Mummy' – as I still call you too.

We two are about as close as we could be; I trust you'd agree.

You raised three boys born within three years, all on your own. In a Housing Trust home, on a low income. You worked six days a week at times, and Saturdays involved driving 25 kilometres to Elizabeth to work in a pharmacy. You didn't have a car in our early years. I think you rode two kilometres to a pharmacy on a bike. Our first car was a second-hand Morris Oxford. It was no limo, but it did the job.

So three boys, spanning three years in age, and Mum, are living in a small three-bedroom place with the thinnest of walls. Dad had left when I was five. My brothers were seven and four. When I was about twelve I was so bad-tempered and combative, you had to arrange for me to go to regular 'child guidance counselling'. This went on for a year or more. Once, I didn't speak to my older brother for six weeks, which is awkward when you're catching the same buses to school and back.

I only raise these things because these are the massive challenges you faced. And almost wholly without considering another partner, for fifteen to twenty years. You just remained solo. At one point you became so understandably overwhelmed, and so near a breakdown, that we three boys had to be shared out to support families while you took two weeks of total rest and recovery. One boy went to cousins. One to grandparents. And I went to the neighbours.

(Thank you Yvonne and Max.)

Our own relationship was strained for six to seven teen years. Only because, it seems, I was struggling with the tight domestic situation, the Dad departure, and adolescence. I moved out as I turned nineteen and things began improving from there, and never looked back. By the time I was 24 I was living interstate and you were lending me small amounts, and I was going to the post office weekly, on payday, and posting you back repayments.

You stood by your sons like a rock. You never once wavered in your complete commitment and devotion to your role. When you could you watched me play football on Saturday mornings at 8.30 – come rain or mud. In six years of school footy my dad didn't see a game. I looked at the other dads and ... pushed on, as we all would.

We four had a Friday night ritual of travelling to Burnside Library. That awakened in us all an appreciation for the magic of books. In my mid-teens you discovered yoga. You then taught yoga for years. And from there you discovered theosophy. You went on to become Australian president of the Theosophical Society, and ended up giving talks on theosophy in Pakistan, New Zealand, India and Australia.

And now we two have shared a common love for theosophy for decades. I've been to the national convention with you and to other TS meetings.

Did you awaken me to theosophy? Or was I going there anyway? My hunch is, and we've discussed this, that we are two like-minded souls who were drawn to each other and were destined to come into each other's spheres. We feel we are two souls who were meant to link up.

You have turned 90 now and you're still living alone and driving. We are all in awe and admiration of your beautiful soul. I love you.

Greg 'That's the Thing About Football' Champion: founding member of the Coodabeen Champions

Dear Mum

What an extraordinary life you've had from humble beginnings surviving poverty, wartime England, the cruelty of your mother and, along with your sisters, the shock of being abandoned by her at such an early age.

You were taken in by your paternal grandmother while your father was a POW. Knowing what I know now, she must have had mixed feelings about this.

I see the evidence of your own mum's harshness – cigarette burns on your hands – and wonder about the depth of emotional scars, as you were left to grow without siblings and a mother's love.

I remember those hands as exceptionally crafty, sewing and knitting the most perfect garments, creating wedding cakes and pies – made before sparrows in increasing numbers for the school tuckshop (and the whole town as word spread).

It wasn't until I was married that you felt you could tell your stories to my husband, in my presence. I never understood why it was so difficult for you to wrap those hands around me until then.

I hated that you were sent in a storm to buy Nana's cigarettes and a young mother stopped you, saying, 'I wouldn't send a dog out in this weather.' That's when the evidence of Nana's frustration was imprinted on your hands.

I particularly love the one about picking up dropped knitting stitches in candlelight for your blind gypsy aunt without her knowing ... Dad says she was the gypsy queen, so she possibly did her knitting with her third eye. He is prone to exaggeration but I relish that it could be possible.

And how your grandmother was against you going out with the young man you met at church. So when you disobeyed her for the first time and married your one true love, turns out, he was the son of the man your mum had run off with when you were left in a hovel and they had emigrated to Australia.

So your mum married Dad's dad! Wish I'd known that when I was growing up.

Both my grandfathers were in the Joe Loss Orchestra before the war and as a child, I shared the piano stool with one, aching to learn how to play. He offered to pay for my lessons and you declined. My passion for music has taken me elsewhere, working with so many talented people, so it's all rolled out really well.

I've lived away from home since I was fifteen, a lifetime ago, and you've given me so much to strive for. While I taught myself to sew, I still haven't mastered zips or buttonholes but am a dab hand at the unpicker!

A couple of years ago when visiting you for Christmas, you nurtured me through a sudden, severe illness – it took a while for me to be well enough to travel back home. I could see it was tough on you – no one wants their adult child moving back in for six months, but I was immobilised! You were supportive, and taught me the healing power of a hug and resilience.

Love you Mum

Sooz xxx

Sue 'Sooz' Camilleri: national music publicist

Dear Mum

I do believe that just about everyone on the planet would have the thoughts I'm having now when faced with the daunting task of thanking one's mother.

How can you put it all into words? Even if I was to write a book about you, I would be worried about leaving something out. There would be thoughts of how amazing a person you were in the face of incredible challenges. How you took it all in your stride, how you never wavered when it came to the raising of us kids.

When we deserved a whack, we got one, when we needed a hug, we got one, and you always had a way with words that will be with me forever.

You never sugar-coated our future, it was always plain talking with a wicked sense of humour.

One of your gems was when I would complain about having to go to school, making up all sorts of reasons as to why I couldn't attend. You would look at me and say, 'Aye you'll go with your lip trembling.'

There's so much more I could say, but I know it would never really describe what a strong and trustworthy person you were.

You and Dad had an enduring relationship that lasted through a lot of rough times. I was so happy to see the good times you both had before Dad passed away.

I placed Dad's ashes underneath that Port Wine Magnolia, but that little tree just found it hard to grow, even losing a few limbs over the years, but when I put your ashes in there, with his, that little tree flourished. It grew and grew and now it flowers every year. Even in death, your influence is there for us to enjoy.

I'm getting too emotional now, so time to close.

You have left behind a great legacy, and our love is undying.

John

John Paul Young OAM: pop legend and ARIA Hall of Fame inductee, Variety Presidential Citation recipient for services to charity

Dear Mum

Although we talk every day (probably too often … and you need to please stop sending me the exact same message in three different message threads, which means I'm getting the same message three times across different platforms; I am, however, really impressed by how quickly you've picked up Instagram and Netflix), there're some things that can get lost in daily conversations that are important to note and have in writing. Big stuff about what it means to be your daughter, and things I'm learning about you as we both grow older.

You're really funny, in every sense of the word. I used to be annoyed by your quirkiness as a kid and just wanted you to be 'normal' like all of my white friends' parents (who were, in hindsight, very boring), but now I know that I'm lucky. Not everyone gets a hilarious mum.

You've been through a lot. I'm 30 years old now – by my age, you had three children and had made a life for yourself in a foreign country. It blows my mind thinking of all the experiences you've endured: a bad marriage, a miscarriage, losing your baby brother to suicide, raising five kids, and leaving behind your entire family and everything you knew in order to build a life in Australia despite never having been here before.

You're very wise. I know a lot of older people, around your age, who can be very proud and ego driven. You used to be like that a bit ... no offence! But you were a typical Asian mum – never apologising for anything, even if you were wrong. These days, if you've messed up, you say 'sorry' and it catches me off guard every time. I'm still getting used to it. You recognise that in life everyone is an eternal student, always learning and growing, and I believe that's real wisdom. I'm really proud of you for that, and I'm proud to be your daughter.

You're a role model. Thank you for always trying your best with us all, even when you were going through a lot of pain and struggling with your own mental health. You've taught me to be a compassionate and kind person, even when people don't always extend that same compassion and kindness to you. You've taught me to always do the right thing, without expecting anything in return. I'm grateful for these lessons, among many other ones, including how to pick the best oranges at the shops, and how to not care about what other people think.

I know there are things you regret and wish you could have done better. I think every person feels that way when it comes to people and things that they care about and love. But we're lucky to be your children. Coen is lucky to be your grandson. I hope I grow up to be as cool as you! (And since

I'm already burping and farting with abandon, like you, and using the exact same skincare regime you've been using for the past three decades, I think I'm already well on my way.)

I love you heaps!

Mic Mic (Baby Horse)

敏儀

Michelle Law: AWGIE Award-winning writer (Sh*t Asian Mothers Say), actor, playwright

Dear Mum

You were there at the start of my life and I was there at the end of yours. In between those two big days were so many moments of love, fear, laughs, tears and lessons.

You sacrificed so much for me. As you aged you felt comfortable stepping back from the business and living it vicariously through me. Always interested in the shows, my 'digs', the travel details, all of it. Your encyclopaedic show business knowledge and experience coloured every comment and observation you made. It was interesting that I worked in such a quickly evolving industry but your observations were always relevant. Seems the more things changed, the more they stayed the same.

For the last twenty years of your life after Dad died, I hope you felt included in my world. I tried to involve you in every event via a phone call or a visit or an outing. I saw you every day I was geographically able. Perhaps that's why when you passed, you left such a hole in my world.

But I know you're with me. And I know you hear me say to you, every day, two simple words: Thank you.

For everything.

Your loving son

Marty

Marty Fields: comedian, actor, musician, session vocalist, author, radio broadcaster, MC, son of Val Jellay

Dear Mum

Over the years you have not only been my mum but my best friend, my accountant, my psychologist and my mentor. You're a passionate but practical woman, who knows the value of hard work and is often guilty of giving too much. I moved away from Queensland 21 years ago, so I am incredibly grateful for our Zoom chats, and that at 77 you're not afraid of technology!

I find myself sounding just like you at times, cursing at my accounting software or talking to my canine mates in the same tone of voice you use. I've even started to see the same wrinkles from smiling, around my eyes and in the corners of my mouth. We share a love of animals, music and cooking, and I'm so grateful for the way you have always supported my choices in life – even when you knew I'd regret them.

We all miss Dad, but oh how much you've achieved these past fifteen years on your own! It has been inspiring. I was overjoyed to see you receive the recognition you deserved last year when you were awarded an Order of Australia Medal for your tireless work for Landcare and the environment.

I'm hoping to grow into a tenacious force of nature like you are and that your sensible financial management might blossom in me too, although much like sewing I've never really taken to it. Most of all, I want to make you proud, the way you continue to make our family proud. You're always our rock and our benchmark. I love you Mum.

Your daughter

Lynette Jean

Lyn Bowtell: multi-Golden Guitar-winning alternative/pop country singer–songwriter (Bennett, Bowtell & Urquhart)

Dear Mum

I remember back to my childhood when I shared the top floor
of our big tall terrace house – my bedroom beside your sewing
room, both of us working side by side, each in our own crazy,
creative mess ... Your room littered with fabric and paper
patterns spread out across the floor, you kneeling perhaps,
holding pins between your lips, the lovely snip, snip, snip sound
as your huge, heavy, metal scissors cut through the fabric.

The thin carpet always scattered with pins – I had to watch
my step in your room. The radio on talkback and your sewing
machine running late into the night, such a comforting sound.
Pages of ideas torn from magazines, the wall a patchwork of
inspiration pinned straight onto Dad's expensive wallpaper!
Projects on the go in every corner – a dress hand-sewn with
flattened milk-bottle caps, or prawn crackers, outfits made of
garbage bags, organza shredded to look like ostrich feathers,
every wardrobe in the house chock full of sequins and
sparkles ... transforming the ordinary into the extraordinary
everywhere you went.

It was like growing up backstage in the theatre, you were always so practical at home in your simple black jeans and T-shirt, so busy you never sat still, always going at lightning speed. Your baked potatoes were the best, if only because you'd turn the oven up as high as it would go to speed along the cooking and they'd literally implode in the heat! Likewise your spag bol that sustained me for days on end, was never meant to be meatballs of course, but you were too busy to even stir the pot. To keep on top of your life, everything had to be made double quantity, twice as fast, loads of washing brought in off the line bundled onto your back the size of a small elephant. Your strength was incredible, your energy unstoppable, your enthusiasm never waned.

And then the nights you and Dad went out, transforming yourself into the most glamorous, larger-than-life being who everyone adored, the house quiet and still after you left, the air heavy with exotic perfume.

The best thing about you as a mum was that you always treated me as an equal, never a child, and taught me all the things you thought of utmost importance. I could affix false eyelashes by the age of six, mix drinks for guests when I could barely lift the bottles of spirits.

And in our house where there were only three of us, Dad being the sensible one most of the time, you were my ally – secretly plotting and planning parties, scheming up crazy ideas with me, fighting banality at every turn!

And thank God we had all those fun times. I always thought we'd get more time together … Little did I know how truly precious my childhood with you was. The last years of your life, eleven years in a bed 'living with Alzheimer's' really sucked for me, mostly because I knew that was never how you would have wanted to live and that was hard for me to live with, but thankfully you seemed blissfully unaware and that was the one blessing that got me through. I just wish so much that you could have enjoyed being a grandmother – my kids you would adore to bits, and they'd make you laugh, I know. We would have had such mad fun together.

But life is a funny thing … and sometimes I think dreams take more than one lifetime to realise. I know you took great inspiration from your Scottish mother, my namesake who I never got to know either. But I know her spirit lived on through you, as yours does through me. And every day I try my best to live by the morals you brought me up to value and hope one day I will inspire my children to do the same – to remember always how precious life is, to follow your heart and aim for the sky, and to prioritise joy and creativity always.

Thanks for being so unconventional, and for being the BEST MUM EVER.

I can say now that I've grown up a bit, that you really were one in a million.

Love your daughter

Katie

Katie Little: writer, singer, comedian

Dear Mum

Thanks for having me. I know that having a fourth daughter would have been disheartening, but apart from my questionable Chinese name,* I never felt that you were disappointed.

Thanks for your wisdom. 'Always have your mad money ready' has been particularly useful.

I wish I had heeded 'Don't mix your drinks' more but I guess, sometimes, you have to learn the hard way.

Your fierceness in protecting your cubs from real or perceived threats or slights was a sight to behold. At four feet eleven inches and 50 kilos, you still managed to control a household of six kids, growing us up into adulthood.

So Mum, where have you gone? Where is that fierce, protective, smart woman?

I dream that you are just playing a game with us and will turn around at any time and say, 'Got you!'

I know you are angry and frustrated with the effort of trying to be 'normal'. I know you are scared of what comes next.

I wish I could help to quieten your mind more and remove that frustration and fear. If it was just a matter of words then here they are, 'Love you dearly Mum.'

Katrina

Katrina Fong Lim: former Darwin lord mayor, Variety NT general manager

* Katrina Fong Lim's Chinese name literally means 'the tail end' or 'last one'. The meaning of her sister's names are 'gold and silver', 'lotus flower' and 'silvery moon'.

Dear Mum

You are such a royal pain in the arse.

Pretty much everything you do is annoying. The way you talk. The way you dress. The way you use words that you think are cool but are actually really cringey. The way you are always hanging around me, like I am some magnetic force. And most of all the way you just stand there in the doorway staring at me, as if I were a butterfly just hatched from its chrysalis, about to stretch its glorious wings and flutter off into the sunset.

Oh, and everything is your fault.

When I can't find my other sock, that's your fault. My bad posture? Definitely your fault. You should have told me to stand up straight while my bones were still setting. That friend I had in high school? Why didn't you notice how bad he was for me and not let me see him? It's clearly your fault my self-esteem took such a drubbing. And where were you that time I was sad but pretending not to be sad so that nobody would notice I was sad and make a fuss?

If only you could have been more there for me. Also, less there.

You're too much. And you're definitely not enough.

How do I know all this, you wonder, and how can I say it so brazenly?

Because my own daughter has bequeathed me the words. That's how.

When she was three years old, she looked up at me, snuggled in my lap, and said, 'Mum, I love you because I am you.'

Now she's fifteen and she growls at me from behind her closed bedroom door, 'Mum, will you just go away.'

It's okay. I know what she means.

Dear Mum, I love you because I am you. And you are me. And we will always be together. Because.

Clare xoxo

Clare Wright OAM: award-winning historian, author, broadcaster, public commentator

Dear Mum

If I was the door – the door to the house –
through which we have all
come and gone and come
since 1970
I could share a lifetime of stories

I would be the door with a handle that shone
out of reach of sticky, pudgy hands
that mother-fingers
tired
with a baby on one arm
would twist open
out
into a rosella-filled glorious garden
and perilously slimy steps
moss covered
autumn-leaf covered
freeing the nearly three-year-old

to the oxide-earthed
crimson-flowered
golden-ashed
wilds beyond

The door through which
at one time
a ten-year-old looked at you
with honesty and reproach
in winter hills damp wet
saying 'I have pneumonia'
(and I did have pneumonia)
and it's only as a parent
that I understand why perhaps you wouldn't have listened
or heard
or acted
on that
and sent that ten-year-old to school sick
infectious
treatment-ripe
for hitherto mustard baths and horse-sized penicillin shots
(and lived to tell the tale ...)

The door through which first boyfriends arrived
sheepish and shy
to a house filled with glorious
odd
eclectic
beauty
and play – such silliness and play
and if they couldn't keep up

or thought we were weird
then back out through the door they left
probably forever

The door that carried the smells of shellac and furniture
polish
sounds of ticking and tacking
banging and nailing
as you restored furniture
and the smell of spray-paint
on the day you created a garden-installation
of impressive magnitude
of golden pumpkins

The door beside which my father
confessed to me he felt suicidal
(I don't think I told you that)
this was before I realised what alcohol can do to a person
before I realised that a person transforms into alcohol's
depressive puppet
before I realised that anything I would or could do
would make no difference
until he left
and never came back

Now the door opens to a house
brim-full
of 50 years of collection and storage
from the sublime to the awful
art nouveau books and lamps
and plastic bags filled with beads and pills and Snoopy dolls

Now when I return home through the same door
grubby-handled and scuffed
with a walking stick (or twelve) leaning beside it
you make a salad that is experimental and delicious
and if I ask for a sailor's suit or a top hat
you have one

Most of all – after coming in
after shifting a shoebox of ephemera from a seat
and clearing a spot on the cedar kitchen table
to rest a teacup
I love sharing
time
space
and your view of the world
as we watch the birds come and go

And I leave again
and again and again
through the same front door
we all do

but that's the thing that door would tell you
that's it's open
and still here

I hope I can offer my children this much

Thanks Mum x

Penelope Bartlau: theatre-maker, writer, installation artist

Dear Mum

There's a collection of childhood photos on the wall next to the bed. Michala put them up, she's good like that. I see you and Dad and Drew every night before I sleep. There's a shot of you holding a baby me. You look amazing, an angel face and a profoundly '70s dress on. We're in silhouette, you are looking at me intently. You're probably wondering what the fuck you're doing with a child when you're not much more than one yourself. Thinking about having your hands full for the next twenty years as I grow up. Wondering what I'd grow up to be, and would I get what I want from life.

I did, because of you and Dad and the way you brought me up – I did.

You cried on the phone the other day. I'd asked you what do you want to do with your life. You said you didn't know, that you'd never known. It's a bugger of a question. It's the great luxury and curse of privilege being asked what you want. Not everyone gets asked it. Not girls like you growing up in Perth in the '50s. I imagine your family didn't know quite what to do with you. These days you probably would have been given a paintbrush, or a laptop with a writing program and told to go for it, explore your feelings. Back then you were medicated.

You were a brilliant mum. Couldn't have been better. You sent us off happy every day. Cleaned us, cooked for us, read to us, loved us, mended us, scolded us, taught us, shaped us. Drew and I turned out pretty well by all accounts. You did that for us. You did that for the family. Now, what do you want to do for you?

As I said, it's a bugger of a question, it's scary, but the answer might be liberating. You got this. We love you.

Love

Toby

Toby Truslove: go-to comedic Australian actor, regular quiz show guest, MC

Dear Mum

You always said you wouldn't move out of your house, that you'd be carried out feet first, and you did exactly that. And now Dad's left it for the last time in an ambulance too.

Dad's in aged care now, that place neither of you ever wanted to be. He broke his hip, and his dementia was too bad. So we had to sell your house, the one you helped him build 60 years ago. The one you grew a marriage and six kids in. You loved that house. You grew up in uncertain times, and had never lived in a house that your family owned. This was *your* house, and *your* garden, and you loved it quietly but fiercely. Like you loved us.

We had to sell it in a rush. There wasn't time for *Remember this …? Remember when …? Remember how …?*

Days followed of thinking – what happened to Mum's favourite vase? That ugly green fruit platter I secretly loved? That picture of Jesus on the lounge-room wall we swore was there to keep us from pashing our dates on the couch? (Okay, we know what we did with that one.) But most of all, it felt like we'd lost you all over again.

You were so *there* in that house, even after you'd gone. Every drawer opened, every cupboard rummaged in – apart from finding weird stuff Dad had hidden, we'd find you: things you'd used, things you'd chosen, things you'd loved. It was still home.

And now it's gone. It's not our home anymore. You'll be pleased to know that a family bought it, not the developer who would've knocked it down and built units. Children will be running around your garden again and messing up the house with love. Just like we used to.

You were the core of our family, the gravitational pull that kept us coming home. We might not come home anymore, but you're still the centre of us. Thank you for being my mother. If life is a lottery, I hit the jackpot.

I love you, Mum. Always

Joanne

Joanne van Os: author of children's books and the bestselling memoir Outback Heart

Dear Mum

How are ya darl?

I know that things have been really tough for you since we lost Dad and my heart breaks every time I think about it. Whenever I get sad, I think of how you are reminded daily that the love of your life was taken away from you too young. I can't imagine how much hurt you must feel every day, getting into a cold bed by yourself.

I'm just so glad that you get so much joy out of most probably your last grandson – our little Colton. He's such a beautiful little boy and he loves his Nanny very, very much. And I know that you love him just as much!

I also wanna say how much I appreciate everything you have done for my brothers and me, and my growing family over the years. You're the sort of person who puts everybody else's happiness before your own. I know this has created situations where you have been hurt and upset, and I just wanna say sorry if that's been the case.

I remember on the farm growing up that you ran the house, you ran all the raising of us. Dad was more or less always at work, but you were always in the kitchen cooking and cleaning, or going up to school to argue with a teacher whenever you thought they were mistreating us or blaming us for something there was no way you believed we'd done! I'll never forget that darl, I never will!

I just love you very much darlin

Shann

Shannon Noll: chart-topping, sheep-shearing Australian idol

Dear Mum

I know I only just spoke to you on the phone the other day, but I thought I'd just drop you a line. It's weird doing old-fashioned things like writing an actual letter. I'm finding I'm doing more and more 'old-fashioned' stuff these days. Stuff like cooking every night, washing my own towels and not just having room service clean my apartment or cabin. Sooooo old-fashioned.

Can you believe my plants are all still alive!!! Thanks for your advice the other day about the fern. You were right, it didn't like where it was in the lounge room. You are most often right you know. I haven't had to ask you how to do things since I was a kid.

I feel like my maturity level on how to do adult things like keep a clean house is at a teenager level right now. I've had a realisation how very spoilt I've been. When I'm on tour with comedy or on set filming somewhere and I reach for my smartphone and just get an Airtasker to clean for me. In the 2020 lockdown I had to do actual cleaning, which made me realise how hard you worked raising us three kids. Wow! You cleaned and cooked and washed clothes and dishes for so many years on your own because Dad was the breadwinner and had crazy notions of it not being his role. Gawd, if Tony didn't do the washing I'd have nothing to wear. So yeah, massive thank you for all you did. You being a Virgo would help I'd imagine. Virgos are so clean and organised. I can't recall you ever having a 'Messy Drawer'. I have several, which I just chuck crap into and close up. I also have a 'Messy Cupboard' and a 'Messy Study'. Out of mind out of sight right?

You have such a lovely face. I didn't really get to have your features did I? Maybe your cheekbones but that's about it. Deborah got your height and olive skin and Jeffrey got your eyes. I got the freckles, gappy teeth, cowlick, and I'm a short arse. Ripped off! But these things do come in handy when you're a comedian.

I think I may have got a few of your personality traits though. I can be quite charitable, and I've always stood up for LGBTQ rights. I remember how you'd have gay boys over all the time, teaching them sewing and cooking. And some even lived with us, if they were having a hard time at home. I really love that aspect about you, and how non-judgemental you are. That must have rubbed off on me 'cos I go that way too now. Remember how Alistair was so camp in his apron, flittering around the house with his makeup on, and how we'd paint his nails? He must have lived with us for around six months I reckon. Remember that time when we were playing dress-ups with him, singing away loudly in the kitchen, and next thing we hear Dad's motorbike in the driveway 'cos he was home earlier than usual, and we had to quickly rub all our makeup off and pretend we were just sitting at the table having a cuppa? So funny, Dad had no idea that most of my 'boyfriends' were actually gay mates of ours. Do you reckon Dad ever knew that we were out at gay bars and piano bars? How did we even get away with that? Did we just tell him we were at the theatre, knowing he had zero interest to ask about our night out? Ha! Townsville nightlife was so great back then. We used to 'do' the whole Flinders Street East strip. To think, the gay bars were all underground back then, but we knew where they were. Remember when I used to choreograph strippers at The Miner's Right? You made their costumes. I loved how I'd come home from school and there'd be drag queens over getting their costumes mended. Dad was none the wiser, he just thought they were for a theatre show that he never went to.

No wonder I ended up on stage. I had your stamp of approval way back, and no matter what I got up to, you had my back. I was actually free to just be myself, half the time. Dad was the other half, where I had to concentrate on my high-jumping skills, softball and learning proverbs.

I have very fond memories of us hanging out during the Annual Magnetic Island Swim that you were on the board of. We had a fabulous weekend away one time and I got so drunk I ended up putting myself plus a moped halfway up a tree. When it looked like I might be kicked off the island, you were so clever disguising me under that massive sombrero to keep me incognito and out of the dangerous position of not being able to keep partying with the swim teams.

Ah Mum, thanks heaps. Thanks for letting me just be myself. Thanks for trying to show me how to be a housekeeper.

But mostly thanks for being so loving, kind and generous and always having my back.

I'll call you over the weekend.

Love from the middle child

Beverley xoxoxoxoxox

Bev Killick: bold and brassy actor and stand-up comedian

Dear Mum

Or Mama, as my Italian blood calls out to you.

A certain unshakeable imagery floods my occasionally excessive imagination, as I sit here and marvel at the incredibly complex life you must have experienced as a young girl. Travelling all that way from a war-torn Italy in the early 1950s, a gutsy six-year-old kid whose fondly remembered father had disappeared a few years prior, to set up a life for his family in Australia.

Six long weeks you endured in the hull of that ginormous rolling ship, a virtual 'ocean-tossed orphan' being passed from hand to hand, while your poor, ailing mama suffered debilitating seasickness. Delivered finally to the cramped and rugged factory-lined streets of Collingwood, with your two mischievous sisters in tow. The three Neapolitan beauties, who would secretly roam the adult-less streets in the after-school hours, eventually gathering gangs of local kids and charging them a couple pennies each to stand on a street corner and watch you box all the wannabe racist youths to a pulp. This image lives deep in my heart as a fundamental detail in the making of you ... and so, of me.

Wholeheartedly fierce, your love is as loyal as any I have ever known. Not only towards cherished family, but for a precious few broken souls along the way, for whom you provided shelter, an ample breast to cry into and plates piled high with crusty bread and pasta. It must be something to do with that authentic Southern Italian blood, the deeply ingrained hospitality mixed with a keen, compassionate intellect that drives your fascination for fragmented characters such as these, both off stage and on.

I have been eternally moved by this particular sense of wonder in you and the translation of that passion into theatre. As a young child myself in the 1970s I was constantly entertained, watching intently as you developed and rehearsed all sorts of wild shows from the hallowed theatre floors of such Melbourne institutions as The Church, The Pram Factory and of course my constant brick-built babysitter La Mama. Now you might be considered a legitimate short arse mama, but that magnificent mouth of yours, that you seem to have so keenly developed on those ancient Collingwood cobblestones, has obviously served as a channel for your boundless creative heart. Not only has it allowed you to move and astonish, with texts as broad and deep as Brecht, Handke, Shepard and Keane, but it has also served as a much-loved teacher, mentor and inspiration to so, so many.

Countless generations of students and collaborators have spoken so highly of you to me over the years, but I'm not too sure just how much you fully comprehend the depth of your constant influence. Particularly the influence you as an artist and a human being have had on me and the unfolding of my creative life. Those totally fucking mad '70s theatrical collaborations, full of sound, fury and wonder, infused me with my very own sense of astonishment and awe, both for the magic of theatre in general and the infinite worlds beyond.

I love you endlessly Mama ... and thank you for loving me so unconditionally.

Damian xx

PS Oh, and cheers for finding Dad too. He's pretty fucking special. And so lucky you persuaded him to barrack for Collingwood ... or Morgan and I might not be here ... ☺

Damian Walshe-Howling: AFI Award-winning actor, writer, director, short film producer

Dear Mum

Happy eightieth birthday.

Sixty years ago this year you married Dad as a blushing nineteen-year-old bride. The partnership has been incredible, even through the very tough times.

You always said you would have a son, Timothy, and a daughter, Belinda. When you were unable to have any more children after giving birth to me, the decision was made to adopt my sister, Belinda.

I will never forget us driving from Sydney to Lithgow Hospital that freezing July morning in 1965 in Dad's old Ford Zephyr, a vivid first memory, even though I was only four years old.

We were that keen that we left home at 4.30 a.m. and got to the hospital at 6.30 that morning.

The matron said there was no way in the world she would release this days-old baby girl from the nursery until the sun had actually risen on that frosty winter morning.

Finally my baby sister was coming home to us. Our family was now complete.

In 55 years, Belinda and I have never had an argument. I think in part because of the love and bond you always inspired and built between us as siblings. Your love of your children has always been equal and without reservation.

When Belinda spoke with you about finding out more about her birth mother, you told her you would be with her all the way on that journey and would stand with her whatever she discovered. That love for your daughter on her quest was without reservation.

The love of your five grandchildren knows no bounds. Their energy and youthful enthusiasm is like a transfusion for you and the family every time we gather together.

The family do understand that love. So much so, that when Nanny says on text or email, 'Dear Family, let's get together ...', we rush to our diaries to save the date.

You are, and have always been, the glue that keeps our family together.

These days, sending your text messages with emojis, surfing the internet and mastering email on your tablet was never a doubt in your mind, or ours for that matter, because you have always pushed yourself to learn new things.

You listening to my talkback radio shows sent Dad bonkers, but knowing you were listening to your son on the radio was, for me, like sitting in the kitchen nattering to you as we have always done, something we always did when I was growing up, albeit now, without the ciggies and the white wine!

There is and has always been one of your wonderful meals on the table, ready to share with you and Dad when I can get back home to see you both. Your corned beef and white sauce is still the best!

I am so lucky to have you in my life today. At the end of every phone call we have these days, as you know, I always say, 'Love you.' You respond, 'Love you too darling.' One day, we both know, we won't be able to make those calls.

Thank you for giving me life. Thank you for being in my life today. I am so lucky.

Love you Mum, always

Your Son Timothy xxxx

Tim Shaw: award-winning Canberra-based journalist, director of the National Press Club, Australia Day ambassador and proud father of three daughters

Dear Mum

I don't remember much about the day you left my dad, only that I didn't want you to go and I didn't want to go with you. I'm told you had to peel me from the tap in the front garden and wrestle me into the car, in front of half the street.

I couldn't adjust to your new lifestyle. It was too different, too fast. And I was an intractable kid.

I wanted you to wear shoes and underwear like other mums and address my concerns about the dope crop in the backyard. I wanted an iron, and a lock on the bathroom door. I definitely did not want a new dad with harem pants and long hair.

Of course, you know all of this, because I found a way to tell you, every day.

It wasn't until I was nineteen with my own baby that I discovered motherhood isn't transformative in the way I thought it would be. Being a mum doesn't erase you. It doesn't replace feelings, fear or ambition. You still have to make hard decisions and you still have to be who you are.

Like you, I took a few hits from the judgement of others. Almost everyone had something to say about my choices, except you. You just helped. And loved us both.

Thanks for stepping up for me so often Mum. I wish you could see the worth in that instead of carrying guilt so heavily. I guess we both know motherhood doesn't work like that. Love

Gill

Gill O'Shaughnessy: journalist from Fremantle and a mum who carries guilt heavily

Dear Mum

There is nothing but silence where you once sat. Dry bones of memory embedded into walls. The crumbling essence of time, from when time was still present. Before it got stolen.

I call you back into being from time to time. Pull up a chair and have a chat with the complex rainbow of your ghost:

Remember when we found that show in some small town with dodgy rides and shitty showbags and you called it Fair Stupid and we laughed until we nearly weed ourselves?

Remember when you fell in love with that antique music box but it was too expensive so you didn't buy it, then Dad secretly asked us to hand over all our pocket money and we put it in an envelope and gave it to you? The look on your face when you opened that envelope.

Remember when I took you to IKEA and you spent $1276.29 on blinds and rugs and throws to make your place look nicer and then I found you there a day later, the things still in their packaging.

The guy at the paper shop couldn't believe it.

'She was just in here,' he said. 'Telling me about her new kitchen linoleum.'

As my siblings and I cleaned up your house, we found:

- a tiny nest of grey hairs woven into the headrest of your armchair
- shards of future hope etched into your diary
- secrets hidden inside eggshells; frail and brittle.

We sorted through your stuff and gave each other pieces of you as gifts to each other. As if hanging onto something you once loved could bring you back.

I got the music box.

Sometimes I unearth it from its precious packaging, and wind it up, and watch the brass roller spin around and around inside its glass hatch, the minuscule needles plucking out a tinkle tinkle of notes which rise high up into the air like tiny brass stars. And sometimes I see a shadow of you rise up with them. An echo of time. A sliver of light. A tiny essence of your DNA wafting up to far, far away.

I'm sorry I couldn't do more to make you happy.

I'm sorry I couldn't do more to make you better.

I'm sorry I couldn't fix you when you were broken.

I wish I'd had more to give you, but –

perhaps these fragments are enough.

Thank you for the life you gave me.

Love

Moo

Mary Anne Butler: multi-awarded Darwin playwright – first (ever) to win the Victorian Prize for Literature

Dear Mum

As your last adopted child, how fortunate I am. You were determined to give the three of us the very best life that we could ever want, and you did. Never spoilt too much but just enough to help me understand that a good life is hard work. A life that is full of love and laughter and a few special things are like the icing on the cake.

As your adopted Aboriginal daughter (in a non-Aboriginal family), you did all that you could to help me understand that I was loved and accepted, and would always remind me that if I ever wanted to take the journey to find my birth family, that you would be there by my side. I did do that, and yes, you were right by my side.

Mum, you were always very proud of my musical ability, and the day I was to be in the school band and missed out, you were horrified, saying, 'But you are gifted.' I said, 'It's okay Mum. They ran out of flutes that day and I was the only one who couldn't be in the band.' You then purchased a brand-new flute and when we marched into the principal's office, you said, 'My daughter is gifted and talented and passed all the exams with flying colours.' The principal was definitely taken aback and as Mum took off her gloves slowly, one finger by one finger, she proceeded to take the flute out of her handbag and ever so gently and strong said, 'So she'll be in the band then?' I did have a great time in the band. LOL.

Mum, you taught me to be strong, brave and resilient. You always said, 'You can be anything you want to be Shell. Reach for the stars.'

And as I received my honorary doctorate from the Sydney Conservatorium of Music this year, all I could see in my mind was you, your love and your hope for me.

'WE DID IT!'

You are my hero Mum. Thank you for all that you have done.

Much love always

Shell

Shellie Morris: proud Yanyuwa and Wardaman woman, multi-award-winning singer–songwriter, ambassador for Adopt Change

Dear Mum

That doesn't feel right. I know I should write Dear Mum but I want to write Dear Genevieve. Even Dear Sally would be more appropriate because that is your actual name. But the fact that you respond to Genevieve is part of the reason why I love you.

With respect, you are the weirdest person I know. I don't know anyone else who can fall asleep during a game and still win it. You're the only person who says 'Corey Baker!' when you're shocked by something. I've checked. No one else says that. I don't even know who Corey Baker is! You have the innocence and faith of a child but you also have the cunning look of a criminal mastermind when a supermarket incorrectly prices a product and has to give it to you free of charge. I've never seen you read anything more intently than a supermarket docket.

I know that you love me. And I feel so lucky that you do. I would understand if you didn't even like me. I haven't been an easy child. First the car accident before I was born – not a great start. Then my crooked ankles and the months of physio requiring you to massage my feet with every nappy change – I was needy from the beginning. Then a career in comedy where I exploited our family for laughs – unforgivable.

But I think the whole comedy thing started because I've been trying to make you laugh my whole life. Making you laugh is my favourite thing in the world. You have the best laugh. The only laugh that even comes close is your mum's and I will be forever grateful that that wise woman gave me you.

I love you and your laugh and your twinkly eyes and your perfect handwriting and I love that I am weird because of you.

Love

Your Sky xx

Susie Youssef: comedian, actor, producer, writer, MC, regular co-host and correspondent on The Project

Dear Mum

I wish you could get one last summer holiday to blast 'All I Want For Christmas Is You' by Mariah Carey twenty times a day from the plastic CD player on the back patio, like it might prevent Hannah and I from sledging each other in backyard cricket, or at least drown out the sound of our festive bickering.

I did the math. You fell pregnant with me roughly a week after social workers delivered a one-year-old Hannah from an Auckland foster home – where her privileged parents were still threatening to kill everyone under the sun – to our run-down hotel in western Queensland, where the working-class publicans had turned upstairs into a sporting academy for half-a-dozen mismatched children who you loved as your own.

I knew that I was a miracle kid, but not that you had recently started taking a shady oestrogen replacement drug – at the age of 38 – from a rogue fertility doctor in the big smoke. (Carmel told me after the funeral.) This is why your seventh pregnancy was the first to make it past three months, and why

Hannah could never remember a time when she didn't have a little brother.

People still say that Hannah and I are spitting images, which is a bit ridiculous, although maybe it has something to do with the way that you used to colour-coordinate our second-hand outfits as if we were identical twins. I think it made us start to walk, talk, smile and laugh the same too, and essentially forget that we weren't related by blood, but knitted together like twine by the kindness of a DNA-blind mother.

I wish that you could get one last Christmas to meet your twelfth grandchild. Hannah called her first kid Lennie, because apparently your name – Lenore – isn't trending in 2020. I wish that you could see the size of the grin and hear the delight in her laughter when Hannah tickles Lennie underneath the armpits, like you did to Hannah and me. Being with them is the closest thing I have to a re-enactment of the 24/7 affection that I was showered with as a baby, the way that you'd check my cot like it was a safe containing a million-dollar bill, and smile at my tears like they were diamonds.

I was the missing jigsaw piece in our DIY family. But I had no idea that there was another way for a mother to be than how you were with us. Or how easily the big, dark secrets of your own past might've produced a hard crust of self-regard and sorrow, rather than the unwavering vulnerability and wonder we received as kids. It's only when you know the unabridged history of someone's struggle that you can truly appreciate the finished puzzle of their happiness.

So I won't get to see you this Christmas, but I'll be smothered with hugs and covered in kisses by Lennie, and I can guarantee for all money that Hannah will be blasting Mariah Carey and

Celine Dion on repeat just like you did. You'd be proud of us, Mum, not because of the designer clothes in our wardrobes or the glittering achievements on our CVs, but because of how much we love each other.

Lech

Lech Blaine: writer, essayist, author

Dear Mum

I was watching a 3D printer the other day, totally amazed at what it could do, when a wild thought struck me – you 3D printed me in your uterus! There I was, impressed at a machine's ability to pop out a figurine, when you zapped together an entire human being. Three of them! You're a certified fucking genius! There aren't enough exclamation points in the world to express how truly epic that is!!!!!!!!!!

The amazement doesn't stop there either. I estimate you gave me 1095 baths before I learnt to do it myself, made me 24 084 meals before I moved out of home (compared with Dad's grand total of six), and lavished no less than a trillion hugs and kisses on me over the years.

My love for music, that comes from you – playing Beatles albums non-stop, singing 'Rocky Raccoon' while letting me make pastry snails from your pie offcuts.

My sense of fun, that comes from you – pulling faces at each other until we laughed so hard we let a little bit of wee out into our undies.

My weird sense of humour comes from you too. Remember that woman who asked what you were going to do with our dog's poo when it shat on the walking path and you said, 'I dunno, I might eat it!'? I say hilarious things like that and people look at me funny too. I don't care, because you showed me that if they don't get you for you, then fuck 'em. (I'm starting to think you should have watched your language around me though. I probably swear a little too much, just like you.)

The point is, Mum, you didn't just compile me out of your stem cells like some kind of biological 3D printer. You loved me. Taught me. Nurtured me. You made me who I am, body *and* soul. Not every kid gets the privilege of having such a wonderful mum. For that, I'm eternally grateful. I know Nat and Johnny are too. They're just not the favourites because they don't say it as often.

Love ya, Mum. Always have. Always will

Tim

Tim Hawken: award-winning writer and favourite child

Dear Mum

Congratulations Loretta! You are the owner, creator and giver of 'The Mum Hug'. Or TMH for the acronym enthusiasts. Of which I am one, they don't call me 'Sam Macronym' for nothing.

I don't really remember the first time I experienced TMH. But I guarantee it was within seconds of me entering this world. My tiny body probably had no idea how much this simple act was going to mean in the years to come. I definitely remember TMH I received as I said goodbye for my first day at proper school. It was a little longer and a lot tighter than the regular ones. And I recall you pulling tissues from your bag as you walked away.

I must apologise, in high school I probably wasn't as receptive to TMH. I even went to some lengths to avoid it. And in retrospect, it really wasn't necessary for me to get dropped off two blocks from school just so others wouldn't see me getting TMH. Only now can I understand how this must've hurt you. Only a fool tries to resist TMH. I promise I'll make up for that.

In my adult life, you've had TMH for every occasion. Always knowing the right one to give me:

- TMH Happy Birthday Edition (Overly enthusiastic, may contain squealing and leave traces of lipstick)
- TMH Sorry You and Your Girlfriend Broke Up Edition (Empathetic, longer in duration and an instant reminder that everything is going to be okay)
- TMH No Apparent Reason Edition (This one happens just because. Sometimes you'll even give five in a day)

I always knew TMH was valuable (with the possible exception of ages thirteen to sixteen when I was more interested in THGIMCH [The Hot Girl In My Class Hug]). But it's the No Apparent Reason Edition of TMH that reigns supreme. TMH conquers all. And I eagerly anticipate the many years ahead of redeeming my lifetime supply of TMH. I'm eternally grateful for the fact that I didn't choose the hug life, the hug life chose me.

I love you with all of my heart Mum

Sam

Sam Mac: **Sunrise**'s *roving weather presenter, columnist, host, ambassador for R U OK?*

Acknowledgements

To all of our wonderful contributors – thank you for your time, for your brainwords and for donating your letters free of charge. Thank you to Shaun Tan for our critters, to Vanessa Radnidge for her continued guidance, to Chris Maddigan and Annie Carroll for always being there, to Jeff Jenkins and Sue Camilleri for sourcing so many great letters, and to Lucy Freeman, the real editor of this book, for her expert stewardship.

And thank you, of course, to all the mums.

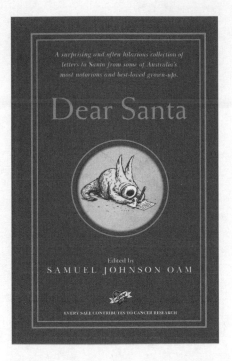

A surprising and often hilarious collection of letters to Santa from some of Australia's most notorious and best-loved grown-ups.

Dear Santa

Edited by
SAMUEL JOHNSON OAM

EVERY SALE CONTRIBUTES TO CANCER RESEARCH

If you could ask Santa for absolutely anything, what would you ask for? *Dear Santa* is a collection of letters to Santa from some of Australia's most notable notables and best-loved grown-ups, including Helen Garner, Adam Hills, Deborah Mailman, Rove McManus, Leigh Sales, Grant Denyer, Molly Meldrum, Shaun Micallef, Missy Higgins and many more. Surprising, entertaining, wicked and witty, this little book of letters is the perfect gift for your favourite human.

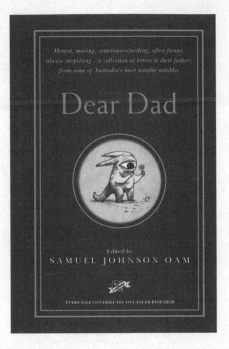

If you could tell your dad anything, what would it be? *Dear Dad* is an honest, moving, emotionally memorable collection of letters to their fathers from some of Australia's most notable notables, including Steve Waugh, Trent Dalton, Samuel Johnson, Kathy Lette, John Williamson, Susie Youssef, Michala Banas, Glenn Shorrock, Joel Creasey, Shannon Noll, Michelle Law, Ben Gillies and many more. This heartfelt, honest and very human book of letters will make you smile and make you cry. It is the perfect gift for the dad in your life.

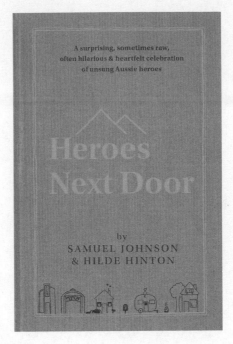

A surprising, sometimes raw,
often hilarious & heartfelt celebration
of unsung Aussie heroes

Heroes
Next Door

by
SAMUEL JOHNSON
& HILDE HINTON

Heroes Next Door is a moving, funny, inspiring
and big-hearted book of true stories that show
how resilience and kindness make a difference,
and that you don't have to travel far to find good
people. Often they are right next door. There are
countless people living quietly in our midst going
over and above to make a difference. People who
face adversity, learn from their experiences and
do all they can to ease the paths of others. Our
unsung heroes who work tirelessly to improve
our lives and our communities without seeking
acknowledgment. These are their stories.

AUSTRALIA

If you would like to find out more about Hachette Australia, our authors, upcoming events and new releases you can visit our website or our social media channels:

hachette.com.au

HachetteAustralia

HachetteAus

loveyoursister.org